ENGLISH SKILLS
FOR UNIVERSITY

Course Book | Workbook | **2A**

Terry Phillips
and Anna Phillips

Published by
Garnet Publishing Ltd.
8 Southern Court
South Street
Reading RG1 4QS, UK

ISBN 978 1 85964 645 8

British Library Cataloguing-in-Publication Data
A catalogue record for this book is available from the British Library.

Production

Project Manager:	Kate Brown
Editorial team:	Kate Brown, Fiona Dempsey
Design:	Christin Auth, Neil Collier, Mike Hinks
Illustration:	Doug Nash, Beehive Illustration:
	(Colin Brown / Janos Jantner / Martin Sanders /
	Laszlo Veres)
Photography:	Banana Stock, Clipart.com, Corbis, Digital
	Vision, Flat Earth, Getty Images, Image Source,
	Photodisc, Stockbyte

Garnet Publishing wishes to thank the following for their assistance
in the piloting of this project:
Lic. Alexia Levi Lovane, Responsable del PII en la Facultad de
Psicología; Mtro. Andrés EscalanteTió, Responsable del PII en el
Campus de Ciencias Biológicas y Agropecuarias; Lic. Kenrick Cornell
Geban, Responsable del PII en la Facultad de Química; Mtro.
Eduardo H. Guerrero Lara, Responsable del PII en la Facultad de
Economía.

Every effort has been made to trace the copyright holders
and we apologize in advance for any unintentional omissions.
We will be happy to insert the appropriate acknowledgements
in any subsequent editions.

Audio: Recorded at Motivation Sound Studios, produced by
EFS Television Production Ltd.

Printed and bound
in Lebanon by International Press: interpress@int-press.com

Contents

Book map

Book map

Unit	Topic areas	Listening	Speaking	Reading	Writing
1 Education	subjects key skills for life education systems	listen and identify words connected with education identifying multi-syllable words from stressed sound predicting: revisions predicting: change of topic learn about History, Geography, Maths, Business and IT	giving a talk about own education giving a talk (1): • *revision of key skills* pronounce vowel sounds use *learn* with a variety of phrases	text type: leaflet with subheading using subheadings finding main V with time clauses finding main V with place clauses learn about History, Geography and Maths	text type: system description spelling vowel sounds the noun phrase: articles present simple vs present continuous adding extra information to a basic SVO
2 Daily Life	ICT regular events/ chores the Internet times	recording advantages and disadvantages understand bar charts learn about digital communication	giving a talk about daily life talking about time giving a talk (2): • *varying expression of information*	text type: magazine article preparing to read: predicting topics learn about the Internet	text types: survey and report silent letters joining sentences with *and* or *but* adding extra information to noun phrase: • *before main N* • *after main N*
3 Work and Business	employment sectors types of job job applications interviews and CVs life skills	transfering information to a table understanding pie charts predict numbers and percentages learn about employment sectors and types of worker	giving a presentation in an interview talking about jobs	text type: article with figures dealing with long sentences (1): • *breaking sentences at and / or / but / because / so* understanding line graphs and block graphs learn about qualifications and jobs	text type: a job application letter spelling with double consonants using articles: *a, an* using patterns: statement + example joining sentences with *because, so*
4 Science and Nature	climate weather animals	predicting from *and, but, or, because* guessing spelling complete the key to a map learn about climate types	taking part in a tutorial about human adaptation to climate adjectives for weather	text type: scientific article using an introduction to predict topics and order of topics learn about animal adaptation	text type: descriptive comparison using comparatives using *only* and *also*
5 The Physical World	structure of the Earth the Solar System continental drift world extremes	recognize key words recognize superlatives using diagrams to record information learn about planets and eclipses	taking part in a discussion about the geology of the continents talking about the past: with day/date; *last* + period; *ago* making sketch maps using adjectives in *how* questions	text type: magazine article with headings and subheadings dealing with long sentences (2): • *introductory phrases* learn about world extremes	text type: description of physical features using superlatives describing size using *be* + *the* + noun to make reversible sentences

Unit	Vocabulary	Pronunciation	Grammar patterns
1	places on campus common verbs describing photographs	pronouncing vowels: revision saying ~ing	*I'm reading a novel about France.* *Are you living at the university?* *What are you working on this week?* *We studied triangles in Maths last week.* *Children learn to read words at six in Britain.*
2	everyday actions everyday objects frequency adverbs	stressing phrases	*I am never late.* *I never come late.* *I sometimes go to a restaurant.* *How often do you visit your parents?*
3	adjectives of personality collocations relating to work possessive adjectives	saying *to* in the infinitive with following consonant stress within words: with change of part of speech	*I'm going to talk about Africa today.* *Are you going to do Geography at university?* *When is she going to start school?* *I would like to work in a bank.* *Do you want to work in a hotel?*
4	conversation openers *like* as a preposition	saying *the*	*Asian elephants are smaller than African elephants.* *Elephants are more protected than giraffes.*
5	the planets prepositions of place and movement adjectives of size and location talking about location: on a page; on a map	saying superlative adjectives	*The nearest planet to the Sun is Mercury.* *Lake Baikal is 640 kilometres long.* *Lake Baikal has a length of 640 kilometres.* *The Himalayas appeared 25 million years ago.*

Unit 1
Education

Key vocabulary

Art *(n)*

assignment *(n)*

Business Studies *(n)*

communicating *(v)*

compulsory *(adj)*

diagram *(n)*

draw *(v)*

evaluating *(v)*

exercise *(n)*

experiment *(n)*

explain *(v)*

flow chart *(n)*

Geography *(n)*

History *(n)*

IT *(n)*

keyboard skills *(n)*

knowledge *(n)*

Literature *(n)*

Mathematics *(n)*

Music *(n)*

nursery school *(n)*

photograph *(n)*

Physical Education *(n)*

pie chart *(n)*

prepare *(v)*

primary school *(n)*

Psychology *(n)*

Religious Studies *(n)*

Science *(n)*

secondary school *(n)*

skill *(n)*

subject (school) *(n)*

text *(n)*

tutorial *(n)*

Lesson 1: Listening

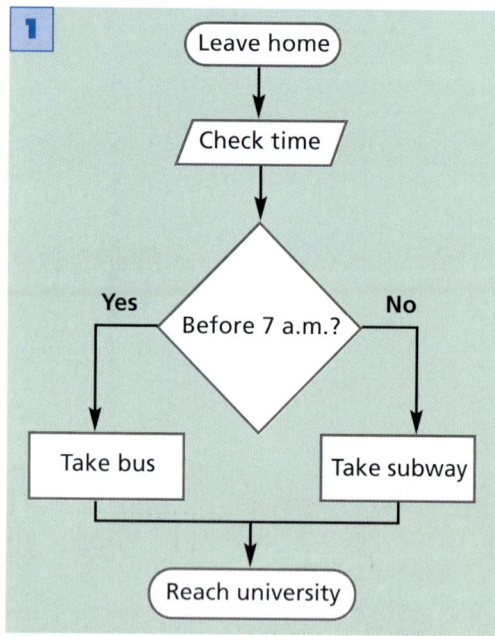

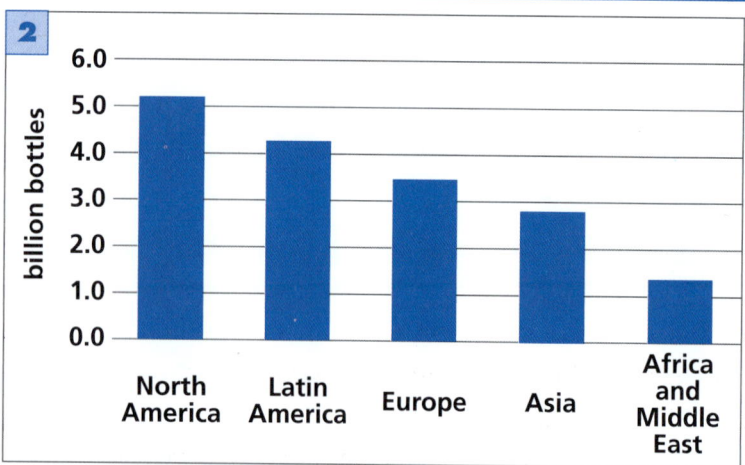

Figure 1: *Coca Cola sales worldwide (2000)*

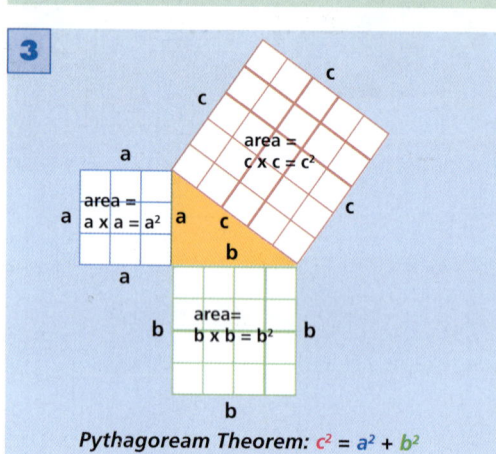

Pythagoream Theorem: $c^2 = a^2 + b^2$

A **Listen and point.** 1:1

Example: *Mathematics*

B **Each picture is from a lesson.**

1 What subject is each lesson?

Example: *1 – IT*

2 Predict some words from each lesson.

Example: *IT – flow chart, computer …*

C 1:2 **Listen and complete the sentences.**

Example: *Look at the flow chart. This is a very simple*
flow chart. It is about travelling to … university.

• listen and identify words connected with education
• identify multi-syllable words from stressed sound
• recognizing change of topic

John F. Kennedy	Italy	$c^2 = a^2 + b^2$
Christopher Columbus	Africa	$C + O_2 \rightarrow CO_2$
The Aztecs	Mount Kilimanjaro	$\Pi = c\,/\,d$
1775	The Moon	area = 1/2b x h
1815	The Antarctic	$E = mc^2$
1914–1918	The Sahara	

D You are going to hear the first part of a lecture about learning.

1 Look at the items above. What sort of information is in each box? 🔘 **1:3** Listen to the introduction to the lecture and check your ideas.

2 Answer these questions.
   a. What do we call all the items in the boxes above?
   b. What else do children learn at school nowadays in your country?

E Listen to the second part of the lecture.
The lecturer talks about the skills below. 🔘 **1:4** Listen. Number the items in the order that the lecturer mentions them.

Table 1: Key skills for life

working with other people	
communicating	
evaluating information	
handwriting	
reading	
keyboard skills	

F Look at the skills in Table 1.

1 Which skills are you good at? Which skills are you bad at?

2 What other skills are you learning at the moment?

   Examples: *I'm learning to drive.*

   I'm learning to write a good biodata.

Skills Check 1

Predicting

• Before a lecture, think:
  What is the lecturer going to talk about?
• During the lecture, think:
  What is the lecturer going to say next?
  Say the word or phrase in your head.

Skills Check 2

Recognizing change of topic

• Lecturers talk about different topics during a lecture. You must recognize the change of topic.
  Listen for numbers. Listen for *next, then, finally/lastly.*

Examples:
*So **first**, what do children learn at school?*
***Secondly**, they learn names and dates.*
*We teach handwriting and **then** keyboard skills. **Finally**, we teach children to communicate.*

Skills Check 3

Identifying multi-syllable words

• In English, words with two or more syllables have one strong sound.

Examples:

1st syllable	2nd syllable
'formula	co'mmunicating
'triangle	e'valuating
'keyboard	im'portant
'knowledge	dis'cuss

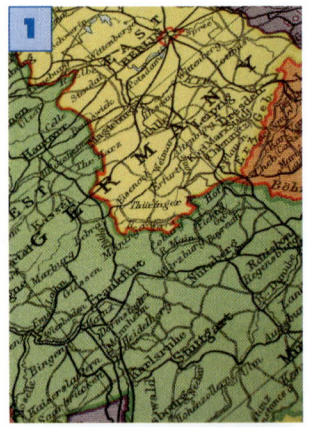

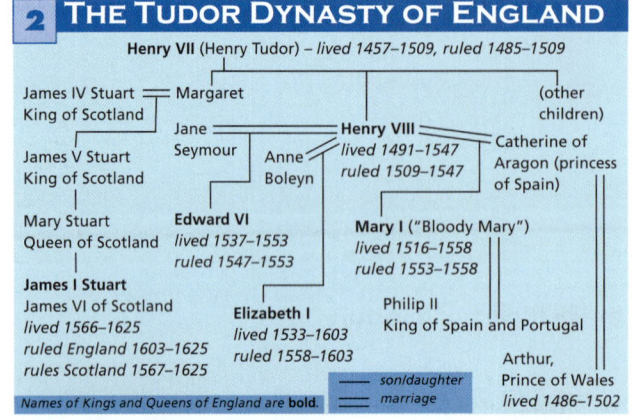

THE TUDOR DYNASTY OF ENGLAND

Henry VII (Henry Tudor) – *lived 1457–1509, ruled 1485–1509*

James IV Stuart King of Scotland = Margaret

(other children)

James V Stuart King of Scotland

Jane Seymour

Anne Boleyn

Henry VIII *lived 1491–1547 ruled 1509–1547*

Catherine of Aragon (princess of Spain)

Mary Stuart Queen of Scotland

Edward VI *lived 1537–1553 ruled 1547–1553*

Mary I ("Bloody Mary") *lived 1516–1558 ruled 1553–1558*

James I Stuart James VI of Scotland *lived 1566–1625 ruled England 1603–1625 rules Scotland 1567–1625*

Elizabeth I *lived 1533–1603 ruled 1558–1603*

Philip II King of Spain and Portugal

Arthur, Prince of Wales *lived 1486–1502*

Names of Kings and Queens of England are **bold**.

son/daughter

marriage

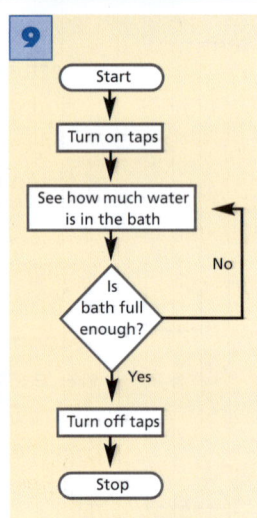

Start

Turn on taps

See how much water is in the bath

Is bath full enough?

No

Yes

Turn off taps

Stop

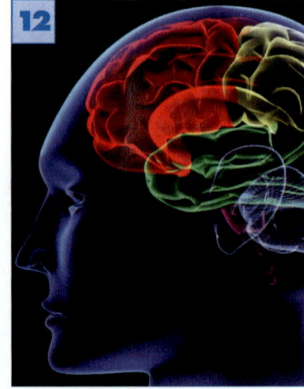

A **Look at the items above.**

1 Name the subjects.

Example: *1 = Geography*

2 🔘 **1:5** Listen and check.

B 🔘 **1:6 Listen to some words. What's the subject?**

Example: *country = Geography*

Pronunciation Check

Pronouncing vowels

• We can pronounce each vowel in English in many different ways.

How do you pronounce the vowels in each of these words?

History	Business
Art	Geography
Education	Religious
Science	Psychology
Music	Studies

C **Look at the conversation.**

1 🔘 **1:7** Listen to the conversation.

2 🔘 **1:8** Listen and repeat.

3 Practise the conversation in pairs.

4 Have a conversation. Give true information.

D **Look at the table.**

1 Write the correct word in each phrase.

2 🔘 **1:9** Listen and check.

learn	to	type
	about	graphs
		draw a graph
		play the guitar
		the Second World War
		write a business letter
		Brazil
		find countries on a map
		use the Internet safely
		spreadsheets

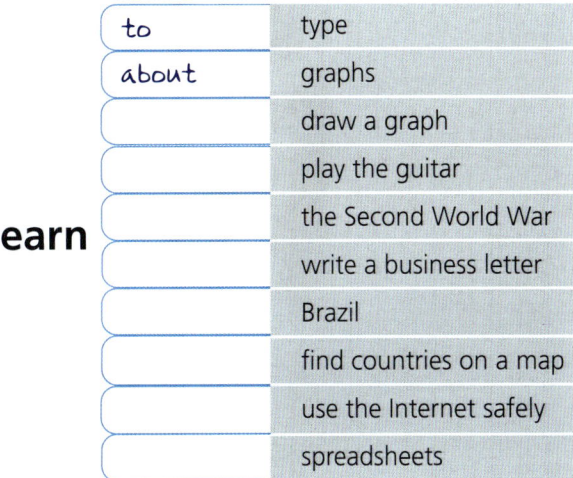

School or university ?
School

? History Psychology Business Studies

History ? evaluate

? → ✓ or ✗

? Psychology

? Important

E **Make true sentences about subjects at school. Use words from the box.**

interesting boring difficult fun easy useful important exciting

Example: *History is interesting.*

F 🔘 **1:10** **Listen to a student's talk.**

Complete the notes.

school or university?	uni. (1st year)
subjects	
learning about	
learning to	
why?	

G **You are going to give a talk about your education.**

1 Make notes.

2 Prepare the talk.

3 Give the talk in pairs or groups.

Skills Check

Giving a talk (1)

Remember!

- Make notes.
- Practise difficult words and sentences.
- Start your talk.
- Stress important words.
- Use good intonation.
- Show enthusiasm – smile!
- Don't read full sentences aloud.
- Look up from your notes.
- Don't speak too slowly or too quickly.
- End your talk.

Lesson 3: Vocabulary and Pronunciation

A **Look at the photos of students on a university campus.**

1 Where are the students in each photo? Use words from the box.

> canteen   outside   laboratory   library   resource centre   park

2 🔘 **1:11** Listen to students. They are describing the photos. Which ones are they talking about?

B **Read the sentences about the photos.**

Complete each sentence with a verb from the box. You can use the same verb more than once. Put the verb into the correct form. Some verbs are negative.

> do   explain   have   listen   look at   point at
> prepare   read   send   sit   smile at   work

1 She's working in the laboratory. She'*s doing* an experiment.

2 Two students are studying in the library. They'_____ books.

3 Two students _____ in the canteen. They (not) _____. They'_____ coffee. They'_____ the camera.

4 These students _____ a presentation for a tutorial. One student (not) _____. He'_____ a text message. One girl'_____ the camera. Two students are working on their laptops. Maybe they _____ some research on the Internet.

5 This student _____ under a tree. He'_____ hard on an assignment.

6 Two students _____ carefully to the teacher. The teacher'_____ something. She'_____ the screen.

OBJECTIVES
• develop vocabulary related to places on campus
• describe photographs
• use the present continuous

C Work in pairs.

Choose a photograph on the opposite page. Describe it to your partner. Which photograph is your partner describing?

D Complete the conversations between two students.

1 1:14 Listen and check your answers.

2 1:15 Listen again. Notice the intonation pattern in each question.

3 Practise the conversations. Use the correct intonation.

A: Hi! Where are you _____?

B: I'm on my _____ to the canteen.

A: Great. I'm going there _____. Can we talk _____ the presentation?

B: Sure. But let's _____ some coffee first.

C: You're studying hard! Are you working _____ your assignment?

D: No, I'm _____. I'm reading the article from the last _____.

C: I read that last _____. It's _____ interesting.

D: It's very _____! Can you explain _____ to me?

E Study the verbs and the nouns.

1 Match the words.

Example: *do some research*

2 Make sentences with some of the phrases.

Example: *I'm doing some research at the moment.*

do	a presentation
explain	a subject
give	a text
prepare	a tutorial
prepare for	an answer
study	an assignment
work on	an exercise
	an experiment
	some research

Skills Check 1

Describing photographs

In some English language exams, you describe a photograph to the examiner in the spoken English section.

We use the **present continuous** to describe the actions in a photograph.

Examples:

*Two students **are sitting** in the canteen. **They aren't** working. They**'re having** coffee.*

Skills Check 2

Using the present continuous

• We use the present continuous:
  1 for actions that are happening now
  2 for actions that are happening around the present time

Examples:

*He**'s having** a cup of coffee. (1)*
*I**'m working** on my computer. (1)*
*She**'s looking** for a new job. (2)*
*I**'m reading** a good book at the moment. (2)*

Lesson 4: Reading

A **Study the text opposite.**

1 What is the heading?

2 What is the subheading?

3 What sort of information is in the text?

- predictions • facts • advice • jokes • news

B **Read the text opposite.**

What advice does it contain? Tick (✓) the advice in the text.

ask lots of questions	☐
ask your friends for help	☐
ask your teacher for help	☐
look at the information again	☐
don't try to understand everything	☐
learn Portuguese	☐
make notes during the lesson	☐
prepare for each lesson	☐
study History	☐
read the information again after one week	☐
try to remember the main points in each lesson	☐
write a summary of each lesson	☐

C **Read Skills Check 2.**

Find and circle the main verb in each sentence below.

1 Before the lesson, ask a question.

2 After the lesson, write a summary of the important points.

3 In Geography last week, I learnt about Brazil.

D **Which kinds of words in English begin with a capital letter?**

1 Tick (✓) the words or phrases below.

2 Write an example of each word or phrase in your notebook.

towns and cities	☐	seas and oceans	☐	names	☐	days of the week	☐
rivers and lakes	☐	countries	☐	study subjects	☐	months	☐
mountains	☐	continents	☐	kings and queens	☐	planets	☐
nationalities	☐	languages	☐	religions	☐		

Skills Check 1

Using subheadings

- Sometimes headings are difficult to understand.

Example:

Make the most of your lessons

- Look for a subheading. Sometimes this is easier to understand.

Example:

How can you learn more in lessons? Here are four ideas.

Skills Check 2

Finding the main verb

- We often begin sentences with phrases of time or place, or both.

Examples:

Yesterday,	
This morning,	we learnt ...
In Geography,	
Last lesson in Maths,	

- Look for the subject and main verb after a comma.
- Sometimes writers do not use a comma in these sentences.

Examples:

Last week in History we **studied** the Second World War.

At the moment in Psychology we **are reading** about memory.

- Find the main verb before you try to understand the sentence.

OBJECTIVES
- use subheadings
- read a text with advice
- find main verb with time clauses
- learn about History, Geography and Maths

Make the most of your lessons

How can you learn more in lessons? Here are four ideas.

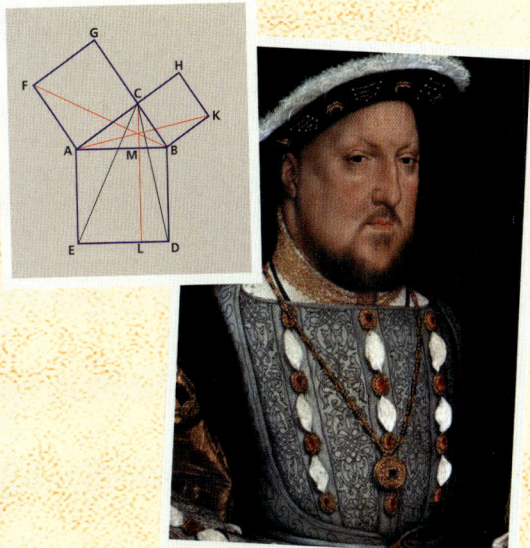

- Firstly, prepare for a lesson. Before the lesson, ask a question. 'What am I going to learn in this lesson?' Look at the next few pages in your book to get an idea.

- Secondly, after the lesson, write a summary of the important points. Then try to remember the summaries the next day. Ask yourself: 'What did I learn in the lesson on Monday?' Be careful with your answer. Don't say: 'We did page 43 in Maths.' or 'We studied the 16th century in History.' or even '*We learnt about Brazil in Geography.*' Those answers are not very good. They answer a different question. They answer the question 'What did I study?' not 'What did I learn?' Study means 'to look at carefully', but learn means 'to know something new'.

- So let's go back to the real question. 'What did I learn in the lesson?' A good answer is a fact, or a way of doing something. For example:

'In History yesterday, I learnt about King Henry the Eighth of England. He was king from 1509 to 1547.'

'In Geography last week, I learnt that most Brazilian people speak Portuguese. Most Brazilians are Catholic. I also learnt that the capital of Brazil is Brasilia. The population of Brasilia is around two million but the biggest city in Brazil is Sao Paulo with a population of more than 20 million.'

'In Maths yesterday afternoon, I learnt to calculate the area of a right-angled triangle. You multiply the base by the height. Then you divide by two.'

- Sometimes you don't understand the information. Here's the third idea. Ask your friends to explain the information to you. If they can't tell you, ask the teacher in the next lesson.

- Sometimes you can't remember the information. So, fourthly, look at the information again after one week.

- One final question. What did you learn from this text? Explain the advice to your partner.

Lesson 5: Writing and Grammar

A One letter is missing from each word.

1 What is the letter?

2 What do you notice about each row of words?

- __sk   b__ll   d__y   m__n
- __nd   b__gin   writ__   teach__r
- l__sten   f__nd   fr__end   g__rl
- br__wn   m__rning   wr__ng   g__
- q__estion   st__dy   __niversity   s__gar

B Complete this text with a suitable article.
Do you need *a*, *the* or – in each space?

In _____ History yesterday, I learnt about _____ Henry VIII of England. He was _____ king in _____ 16th century, from _____ 1509 to _____ 1547. In _____ Geography, I learnt that _____ most Brazilian people speak _____ Portuguese. I also learnt that _____ capital of _____ Brazil is _____ Brasilia. _____ population of _____ Brasilia is around two million, but _____ biggest city in _____ Brazil is _____ São Paulo, with _____ population of more than 20 million. In _____ Maths yesterday afternoon, I learnt to find _____ area of _____ right-angled triangle. You multiply _____ base by _____ height. Then you divide by two.

C Look at the grey boxes and the green boxes.

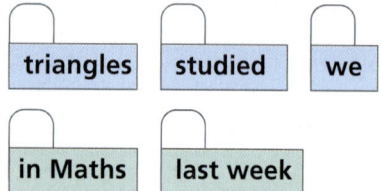

1 Number the grey boxes in order. Where can you put the green boxes?

2 Copy the words to make sentences. Remember punctuation.

D Write three sentences about your studies.

Skills Check 1

Spelling vowel sounds

Remember!
We can spell **different vowel sounds** with **the same vowel letter.**
Examples:

letter	sounds
a	ask, ball, day, man
e	end, begin, teacher
i	listen, find, girl
o	brown, morning, wrong, go
u	question, study, university, sugar

Skills Check 2

The noun phrase (1)

Remember!
We often need an article with a noun.
Examples:

article	noun
a	triangle
	person
	subject
an	idea
	apple
	exercise
the	capital
	king
	height

But sometimes, we do not need an article.
Examples:

In **History** yesterday, …
I learnt about the king of **England**.
I learnt that most Brazilian **people** …
The biggest city is **São Paolo**.

OBJECTIVES
- spell vowel sounds
- grammar: the present continuous
- study the noun phrase: articles

E **Look at Table 1.**

When do we use this pattern? Tick (✓) one or more situations.

to talk about actions at the moment	☐
to talk about past events	☐
to talk about actions around now	☐
to talk about habits	☐

Table 1: *Subject + Aux (+ not) + Verb (= Other)*

S	Aux		V	Other
I	am 'm		reading	a novel about France.
He	is 's	not n't	writing	a letter.
She			waiting	in her office.
We	are 're		learning	about Brazil now.
They			working	at the moment.

F **Look at Table 2. Compare it with Table 1.**

1 How do we make *yes/no* questions with this pattern?

2 How do we make answers? Guess!

Table 2: *Aux + Subject + Verb (= Other) + ?*

Aux	S	V	Other
Are	you	living	at the university?
Is	he	studying	Psychology.
	she	doing	an experiment?
Are	we	doing	Exercise B?
	they	working	at the moment?

G **Look at Table 3. Compare it with Table 2.**

1 Complete each question.

2 How do we make *wh~* questions with this pattern?

3 Work in pairs. Ask about your partner's studies this week. Use *yes/no* and *wh~* questions.

4 Write about your partner's studies this week.

Table 3: *Q-word + Aux + Subject + Verb (+ Other)*

Q word	Aux	S	V	Other
What	are	___	reading	?
		___	doing	at the moment?
	is	___	studying	now?
		___	working on	this week?

H **Present simple or present continuous?**

Study the sentences and questions below.

1 Which tense has the auxiliary *is* or *are*?

2 Which tense has the auxiliary *do* in questions and negatives?

3 When do we use the present simple?

4 When do we use the present continuous?

Present simple	Present continuous
Children study English at primary school in some countries.	The children are studying English at the moment.
Children don't learn to read at nursery school in Britain.	The children aren't studying French.
Do children study English at primary school in your country?	Are the children studying English at the moment?
What do children study at primary school?	What are the children doing?

I **Complete each sentence. Use the words in brackets.**

1 She lives at home, but this week (stay / friends) <u>she is staying with friends</u>.

2 I have coffee most mornings, but this morning (tea) …

3 He doesn't usually read novels, but at the moment (*War and Peace*) …

4 They usually do assignments together, but this time (alone) …

Lesson 6: Writing and Grammar

nursery

to share toys

primary school

to read

secondary school

to use the Internet

A **Look at the photographs above.**

1 What age do people start and finish each school in your country?

2 What **skills for life** do children learn at each school in your country? Write some words under each school.

3 Which **subjects** are compulsory at secondary school in your country? In other words, which subjects do all children study?

B **Look at the grey boxes and the green boxes.**

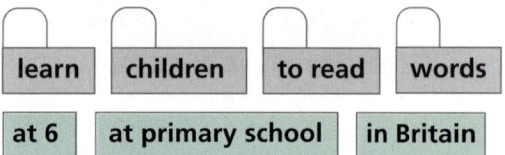

1 Number the grey boxes in order. Where can you put the green boxes?

2 Copy the words to make sentences. Remember punctuation.

3 Make more sentences with the same pattern. These sentences should be about your country. Think of new items for each box.

C **Write about things you have learnt. Add the extra words in different places.**

Examples: *I learnt to read stories at 7.*

At 17, I learnt to drive a car.

D Read the sentences. (Circle) the correct word or phrase in each case.

1	Are you	work / working	at the moment?
2	What	you are / are you	doing in IT this term?
3	In your country,	do children study / are children studying	a foreign language at primary school?
4	When	do children learn / children learn	to read in Mexico?
5	I like English because	is useful / it is useful	in your life.
6	Last week, we learnt	drawing / to draw	graphs.
7	We learnt	of / about	flow charts yesterday.
8	IT is not	a subject compulsory / a compulsory subject	at secondary school in Germany.

E Read about Australia. Complete the Australia column of Table 1 with the correct information.

F Read the notes about Germany. Write three paragraphs.

G Make notes about your country. Write three paragraphs about your country.

Table 1: *Education in Australia and Germany*

		Australia	Germany
Stages	nursery		3–6
	primary		6–10
	secondary		10–19
Subjects at secondary school			Ger., His., Maths, Sci., PE, a for. lang. = Fr., Eng. IT = not compul.
Knowledge			imp. facts about Ger., Eu. and the world
Skills			skills for life, e.g., eval. inf.

Education in Australia

In Australia, children start nursery school at three. They stay for two years. At five, they go on to primary school. Primary school lasts seven or eight years. At 12 or 13, they start secondary school. They finish secondary school at 18.

At secondary school, there are six compulsory subjects. All students study English, IT, Mathematics, Science and Physical Education. They also study a foreign language. They can choose Japanese, French, German or Chinese. Religious Studies is not a compulsory subject.

Australian students learn knowledge and skills at school. They learn important facts about Australia, Oceania and the world. They also learn skills for life. For example, they learn to work with other people.

Grade your progress (1 = poor to 5 = very good)

At the end of Unit 1, I can:

☐ listen and identify words connected with education

☐ give a talk about own education

☐ use the present continuous with good pronunciation

☐ use headings and grammatical features to read texts more easily

☐ write sentences with a variety of word order

☐ use the grammar of the unit accurately

Transfer

Find opportunities to talk about what you have learnt in other subjects using English.

Reflect

Think about the activities you did in this unit. Which ones did you find most enjoyable? Which ones did you find most useful? Think about your own place in the learning process and how you can affect the outcome.

Unit 2
Daily Life

Key vocabulary

digital communication
cellphone *(n)*
laptop *(n)*
mp3 player *(n)*
social networking site *(n)*
texting *(v)*
voice call *(n)*
website *(n)*

daily routine
brush my hair *(v)*
brush my teeth *(v)*
catch the bus *(v)*
get dressed *(v)*
get home *(v)*
get up *(v)*
go to bed *(v)*
go to sleep *(v)*
have a shave *(v)*
have shower *(v)*
leave home *(v)*
lock the door *(v)*
pack my bag *(v)*
put on make up *(v)*
wake up *(v)*

frequency adverb
always *(adv)*
never *(adv)*
often *(adv)*
sometimes *(adv)*
usually *(adv)*

others
advantage *(n)*
alarm *(n)*
disadvantage *(n)*

Lesson 1: Listening

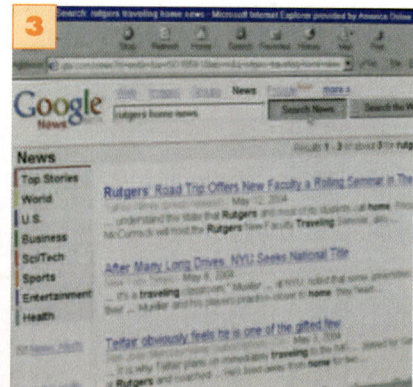

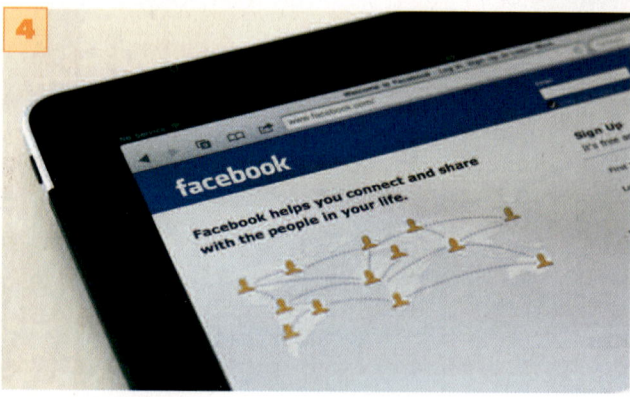

A 🔘 **1:16 Listen and point.**

Example: *a cellphone*

B 🔘 **1:17 Listen to the first part of a Sociology lecture.**

What digital methods do teenagers use for:

- communication?
- entertainment?
- research?

C 🔘 **1:18 Listen to the next part of the lecture. What does the lecturer say about teenagers? Tick (✓) one or more sentences.**

1	They talk a lot on the phone.	
2	They talk a lot face-to-face.	
3	They send a lot of text messages.	
4	They communicate in the same way as their parents.	
5	They use digital methods more than their parents.	

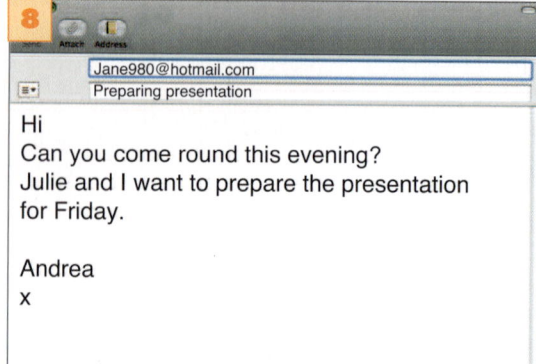

OBJECTIVES
• record advantages and disadvantages
• understand bar charts
• learn about digital communication

D Study the bar chart in Figure 1.

🔘 **1:19** Listen to the next part of the lecture. Write the number of minutes next to each bar.

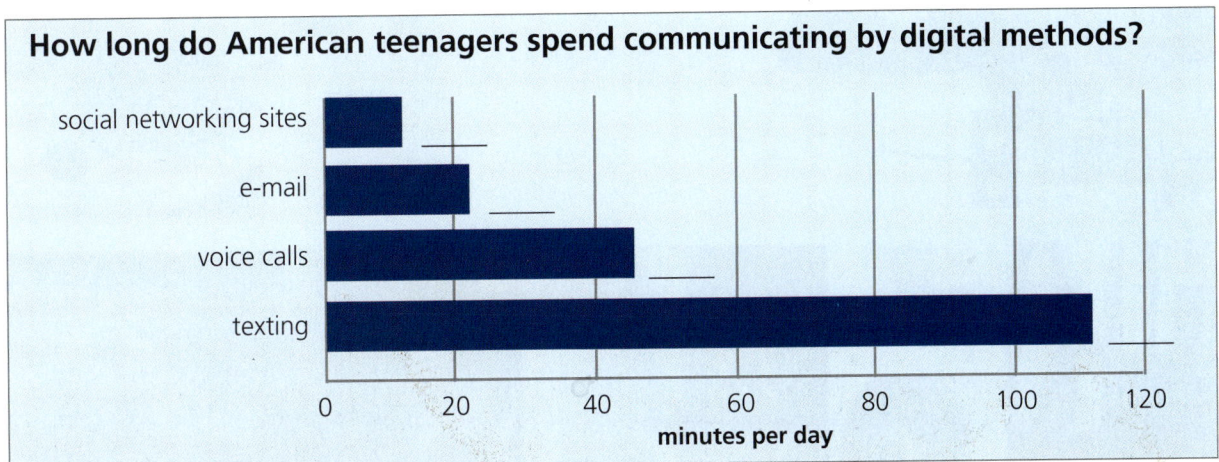

Figure 1: *American teenagers and digital methods of communication*

E In the final part, the lecturer talks about communicating by digital methods.

1 🔘 **1:20** Listen and make notes in Table 1.

2 What do you think? Are digital methods of communication a good thing or a bad thing?

3 🔘 **1:21** Listen to the whole lecture. Follow the lecture in the tapescript.

F How long do you spend communicating by digital methods every day, on average?

1 Complete the bar chart in Figure 2.

2 Compare your bar charts in groups.

Skills Check

Recording advantages and disadvantages

• Sometimes lecturers talk about advantages and disadvantages. Record your notes in a table.

Table 1: *Digital communication: advantages and disadvantages*

advantages	disadvantages

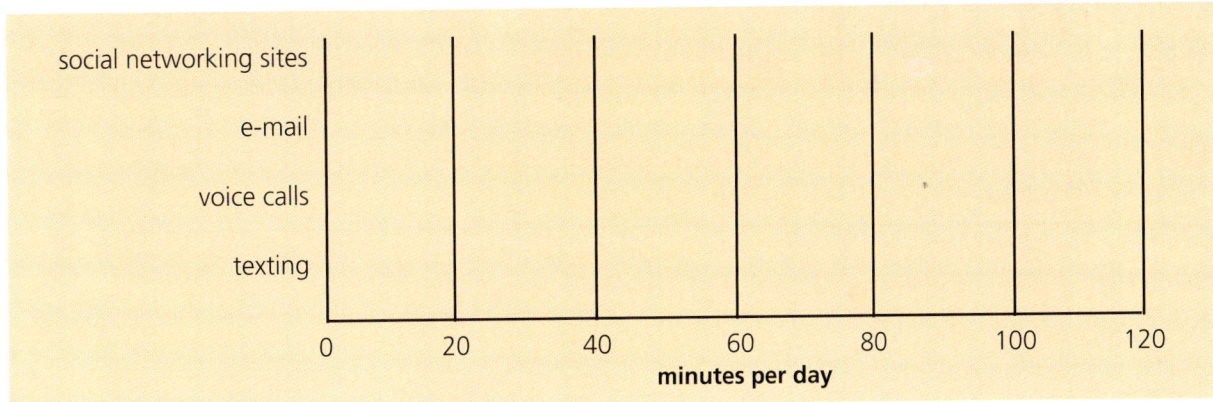

Figure 2: *My use of digital methods of communication*

Lesson 2: Speaking

A Look at the photographs of actions from daily life. Match the verb phrases in the box to the photographs.

> catch the bus   get home   get up   go to bed   go to sleep   leave home
> have a meal   have a sandwich   have breakfast   listen to lectures (x2)   wake up

Example: *1 wake up*

B What time do you do each action? Work in pairs. Tell your partner.

Example: *1 I wake up at 7.30.*

- talk about time
- give a talk about daily life
- vary sentence patterns

C 1:23 **Listen to a talk by a university student in China. Make notes in a table like this.**

time	action	digital communication
6.30	wake up, get up	turn on cellphone; get text messages

D **You are going to give a talk about your daily life.**

1 Make notes in a table like this.

2 Practise sentences for your talk.

time	action	digital communication
7.30	wake up	use the alarm on my cellphone

E **Give your talk in groups.**

Listen to the other students in your group.
Do they do anything different from you?
Make some notes.

Skills Check 1

Talking about time

- We can talk about time in two ways.

Examples:

seven fifteen	quarter past seven
eight thirty	half past eight
nine forty	twenty to ten
two forty-five	quarter to three

1:22 Listen to some times.
Write the time in digital form.
Draw a clock face with the same time.

Example:
six fifteen

Skills Check 2

Giving a talk (2)

- Sometimes several sentences in a talk have the same basic pattern.

Examples:
I wake up at 7.00.
I get up at 7.15.
I have breakfast at 7.30.
I leave home at 8.00.

Try to find different ways to say similar information.

Examples:
I wake up at 7.00.
At 7.15, I get up.
I have breakfast at half past seven.
I leave home half an hour later.

A **Look at the photographs above. They show parts of the morning routine for many people.**

1 Name each activity. Choose a verb from the left box and a phrase from the right box.
You can use one verb twice.

Example: *get dressed*

2 🔘 **1:24** Listen and check your answers.

3 What is the opposite of these actions?

a. get dressed

b. pack my bag

c. lock the door

d. put on make up

brush	a shave
clean	a shower
get	dressed
have	my bag
lock	my hair
pack	my make up
put on	my teeth
	the door

B **Work in pairs.**

1 Do you do all the actions in the photographs every morning? What order do you do the actions in?
Tell your partner.

Example: *First, I clean my teeth. Then I have a shower.*

2 What order do you do the actions in the afternoon/evening? Tell your partner.

Pronunciation Check

Stressing phrases

We often put the main stress on the object in a sentence.

Examples:

I have a shower.

I clean my teeth.

🔘 **1:25** Listen and practise.

OBJECTIVES
- develop vocabulary related to everyday items
- stress phrases correctly
- talk about regular events with frequency adverbs

C **Look at the conversation.**

1 🔘 **1:26** Listen.

2 🔘 **1:27** Listen and repeat.

3 Ask and answer. Give true information.

4 Talk about your partner.

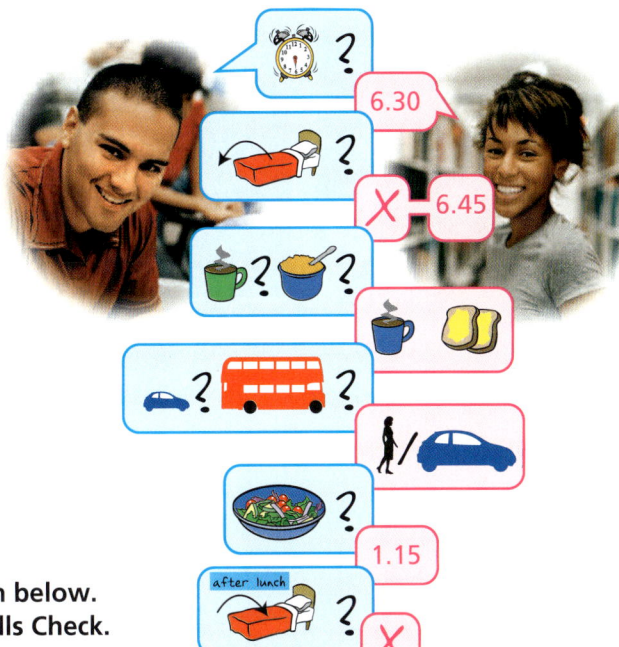

D **Complete the frequency adverbs.**

100%	al_____
75–90%	us_____
60–75%	of_____
20–30%	so_____
0%	ne_____

E **There is one mistake in each sentence or question below. Find the mistake and correct it. Then read the Skills Check.**

1 I am happy always. _always happy_____

2 Never he goes to the sports centre. _____

3 She sometimes is kind. _____

4 They ask often lots of questions. _____

5 We usually having dinner at 8.00 p.m. _____

6 How do you often get to university? _____

7 Do you eat ever in a restaurant? _____

8 When often do you have takeaway food? _____

F **Study the words in the columns.**

1 Match the words to make time and frequency phrases.

a.	every	a week
b.	most	day
c.	at	days
d.	on	Fridays
e.	in	the evening
f.	twice	the weekend
g.	three	times a week

2 Make new phrases with each pattern.

Examples: *every month, most weeks*

G **Work in pairs.**

Talk about your routine. Use frequency adverbs from Exercise D and time and frequency phrases from Exercise F.

Example: *I always have sandwiches at lunchtime.*

Skills Check

Talking about regular events

- We often talk about regular events with frequency adverbs. Notice the position of the adverbs with *be* and with other verbs.

Examples:

I	am	**always**	late.
He	is	**usually**	first.
She		**often**	angry.
We	are	**sometimes**	tired.
They	are	**never**	happy.

I	**always**	come	late.
He	**usually**	comes	first.
She	**often**	gets	angry.
We	**sometimes**	feel	tired.
They	**never**	look	happy.

- We can ask about regular events with *usually*, *ever* and *often*.

Examples:

*When do you **usually** get up?*
*Do you **ever** sleep in the afternoon?*
*How **often** do you go to bed late?*

Lesson 4: Reading

A **You are going to read the text opposite.**

1 What should you do before you read the text?

2 Read the Skills Check and check your ideas.

B **Prepare to read the text opposite.**

1 Read the title and the first paragraph. What information will be in the text? Tick (✓) one or more items.

a.	how to use the Internet
b.	the history of the Internet
c.	bad things about the Internet
d.	good things about the Internet

2 Read the section headings. Which section will contain each of the words below? Write *R*, *C* or *SL*:

a.	clubs	_SL_	e.	information	___
b.	e-mail	___	f.	instant message	___
c.	Facebook	___	g.	library	___
d.	Google	___	h.	telephones	___

C **Read the text opposite. Answer the questions.**

1 Before the Internet, how did people:

a. do research?

b. communicate with people in another town or another country?

c. meet people with similar interests?

2 How can you do the things above now?

D **Match each word or phrase from the text with a definition on the right.**

1	reference book	a lot of money
2	librarian	camera on a laptop or PC
3	expensive	information about a person
4	webcam	make for the first time
5	create	person working in a library
6	profile	book with factual information

Skills Check

Preparing to read

• Before you read a text:

1 Look at any **illustrations**.

2 Read the **title**.

3 Read the **introduction** or **first paragraph**.
Stop. Think:
What information will be in the text?

4 Read any **section headings**.
Stop. Think:
What information will be in this paragraph?

This is called **prediction**.
Perhaps your predictions are right.
Perhaps they are wrong. But your predictions will help you to understand the rest of the text.

OBJECTIVES
- prepare to read: predict topics
- read a text with a point of view
- learn about the Internet

The Internet

Is it good or bad? (Part 1)

The Internet is now an important part of our lives. But is the Internet a good thing or a bad thing? This week, we look at the good side of the Internet. We consider three areas. Firstly, we look at the Internet and research. Secondly, we think about the Internet and communication. Finally, we consider the Internet and social life.

Research

Before the Internet, people used their own books to do research, or they went to a library to borrow them. With reference books, you had to sit in the library. You made notes from the books. You could not take the books home. Nowadays, you can sit at home or you can sit in the resource centre at school. You can find information on the Internet.

Before the Internet, you looked up subjects in an index. Then you asked the librarian for the book. Nowadays, you just type a question or some words into the search box of a website such as Google or Yahoo.

Before the Internet, you could only look at a small number of books for research. Nowadays, sites like Google search hundreds of thousands of websites. They often give you hundreds of results.

Communication

Before the Internet, you wrote letters or you telephoned people. Letters took a long time. Telephones were in people's houses. Sometimes the person was not at home. Telephone calls were expensive. Nowadays, you just send an e-mail or write an instant message on MSN. The message arrives in seconds. It goes to the person, not the person's home. It does not cost anything at all. You can even see each other if you have webcams.

Social life

Before the Internet, it was difficult to find people with similar interests. People joined clubs or they bought specialist magazines. Nowadays, there are many websites, such as Facebook. Just create your own profile. People with the same interests will contact you.

Next week: *The bad side of the Internet.*

Lesson 5: Writing and Grammar

A **Study the extracts.**

1 What do the highlighted words have in common?

2 Read Skills Check 1.

3 Find the extra information in each extract **before** the main noun.

4 Read Skills Check 2.

5 Find the extra information in each extract after the main noun.

an important **part** of our lives

the search **box** of a website

the resource **centre** at school

a small number of **books** for research

an instant **message** on MSN

B **Choose a word or phrase from the box to go in front of each noun below. Write the noun phrases.**

| biggest instant compulsory digital foreign |
| important ~~primary~~ real seven thousands of |

Example:

1 a school   _a primary school_
2 years   _____
3 the facts   _____
4 a subject   _____
5 a language   _____
6 the question   _____
7 the city   _____
8 results   _____
9 communication   _____
10 message   _____

C **Make noun phrases from the words in each box. Write the noun phrases.**

Example: *students at university*

a book	about psychology
a country	at university
a part	in Asia
a website	in Geography
an interest	in primary schools
children	of a triangle
students	of Brazil
teachers	of History
the area	of the city
the population	on the Internet

Skills Check 1

The noun phrase (2)

- We sometimes add **extra information before** the **main noun** in a noun phrase. The extra information is usually another **noun**, an **adjective** or a **quantity**.

Examples:

main noun	with extra information
the **life**	the **daily** life
their **phones**	their **cell**phones
students	**most** students

Always find **the main noun** in a noun phrase. Then look at **the extra information before** the noun.

Skills Check 2

The noun phrase (3)

- We sometimes add **extra information after** the **main noun** in a noun phrase. The extra information often follows a **preposition**.

Examples:

main noun	extra information
the **life**	**of** students
1,000 **students**	**at** university
more **students**	**in** the survey

Always find **the main noun** in a noun phrase. Then look at **the extra information** before and/or after the noun.

D **Look at all the tables.**

Complete the tables with one word in each space.

E **Look at Tables 1, 2 and 3.**

1 Where do you put the frequency adverbs below? Position 1, 2, 3, 4, (5)?

- always _____
- usually _____
- often _____
- never _____

2 What about this frequency adverb?

- sometimes _____

F **There is one mistake in each of these frequency phrases. Find it and correct it.**

1 every days

2 most day

3 one time a week

4 twice week

5 three time a week

G **Look again at Tables 1 and 3.**

Where can you put the frequency phrases in Exercise F? Position 1, 2, 3, 4, (5)?

H **Look at Table 4 for one minute. Then close this book and draw the table in your notebook.**

I **Write about regular events in your life. Write true sentences with sentence patterns from this lesson. Use a frequency adverb or phrase.**

J **Work in pairs. Ask and answer questions about regular events.**

Use question patterns from Table 4 and sentence patterns from Tables 1, 2 and 3.

Table 1: *Subject + Verb (to be) + Adjective with frequency adverbs*

1	Pronoun	2	Verb	3	Adjective	4
	I		_____		late.	
	You		_____		tired.	
	He		_____		ill.	
	She		is		_____.	
	They		are		_____.	

Table 2: *Subject + Verb + Objective (+ Other) with frequency adverbs*

1	S	2	V	3	O	4	Other	5
			visit		_____		at weekends.	
	I		meet		_____		on Fridays.	
			_____		college work		in the afternoon.	
			play		sports		_____.	

Table 3: *Subject + Verb + Preposition (+ Noun) with frequency adverbs*

1	S	2	V	3	Prep	4	Other	5
			_____		in		a restaurant.	
			_____		_____		the library.	
	I		go				pray.	
			listen		_____		_____.	
			write				my parents.	

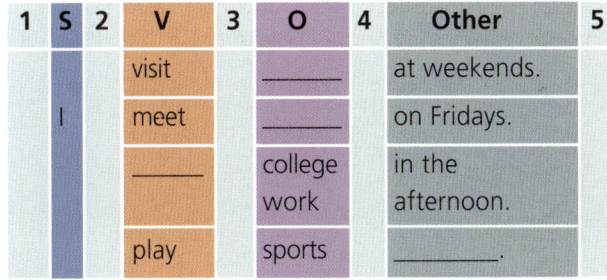

Table 4: *Q-word + Aux + Subject + Verb (+ Other)*

Q word	Aux	Pronoun	Verb	Noun
How _____			visit	your parents?
When	do	you	do	_____?
_____			_____	at weekends?

Lesson 6: Writing and Grammar

A **Study the words below.**

1 What do they all have in common?

2 Read Skills Check 1.

3 Write the words with the correct spelling.

a. anser   *answer*

b. assinment   _____

c. busness   _____

d. diffrent   _____

e. evning   _____

f. frend   _____

g. intrest   _____

h. nowledge   _____

i. laboratry   _____

j. lisen   _____

k. litrature   _____

l. Mathmatics   _____

m. mountins   _____

n. ofen   _____

o. refrence   _____

p. rite   _____

B **Read the text below about the daily lives of university students.**

1 Choose the best joining word in each case.

2 What do the underlined pronouns refer to in each sentence?

University students in the digital world

Researchers in Britain recently looked at the daily life of university students. <u>They</u> talked to 1,000 students at university *and / but* they asked <u>them</u> about their use of digital communication.

Most students in the survey never turn off their cellphones. <u>They</u> are always on during face-to-face meetings *and / but* <u>they</u> are always on during mealtimes. The students always answer their cellphones during face-to-face meetings *and / but* <u>they</u> always answer <u>them</u> during mealtimes. The cellphones are sometimes on during lectures *and / but* <u>they</u> are usually on silent.

The students always listen to their mp3 players on their way to and from university *and / but* <u>they</u> never listen to <u>them</u> during lectures.

The students sometimes communicate with their friends by voice calls and by e-mail *and / but* <u>they</u> usually communicate with <u>them</u> by text message.

C **Read the sentences. Circle the correct word or phrase in each case.**

1	I never am / I am never	late for college.
2	He plays sport often / He often plays sport.	after college.
3	They	eat in the restaurant often. / often eat in the restaurant.
4	Sometimes I visit / I visit sometimes	my parents at the weekend.
5	I	every day pray. / pray every day.
6	We study	every afternoon in the library. / in the library every afternoon.
7	I eat in a restaurant	one time a week. / once a week.
8	She writes to her parents	every weeks. / every week.
9	How usually / How often	do you study at weekends?
10	What you do / What do you do	most evenings?

D **Do a survey. Write about your results.**

1 Ask ten people in your group the questions in Table 1 below. Mark their answers under (**A**)lways, (**U**)sually, (**O**)ften, (**S**)ometimes or (**N**)ever.

2 Write a short report about your results (see the report in Exercise B). Use pronouns. Join sentences with *and* and *but*.

Table 1: *Use of digital communication in my group*

		A	U	O	S	N
Do you turn off your cellphone …	during face-to-face meetings?					
	during lectures?					
	during mealtimes?					
	at night?					
Do you listen to your mp3 player …	during face-to-face meetings?					
	during lectures?					
	during mealtimes?					
	on your way to and from university?					
Do you communicate with your friends …	face to face?					
	by voice calls?					
	by text messages?					
	by e-mail?					
	through a social networking site?					

At the end of Unit 2, I can:

- ☐ listen and identify advantages and disadvantages

- ☐ give a talk about daily life

- ☐ use stress appropriately in sentences

- ☐ use illustrations, titles, headings and text introductions for prediction

- ☐ make compound sentences using *and* and *but*

- ☐ use the grammar of the unit accurately

Transfer

Start reading in English. You can look at online magazines such as *Inspiration Lane* at http://www.inspirationlane.blogspot.com/

Reflect

One difference between English and Spanish is that there is no direct relationship between spelling and pronunciation in English. Take an interest in these differences by collecting and thinking about unusual spellings. Make a start by noticing the words that have silent letters such as *answer* and *know*.

Unit 3
Work and Business

   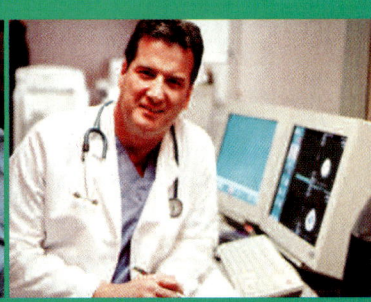

Key vocabulary

achievement *(n)*
advertisement *(n)*
agriculture *(n)*
applicant *(n)*
application *(n)*
background *(n)*
bank *(n)*
bank clerk *(n)*
boring *(adj)*
builder *(n)*
bus *(n)*
bus driver *(n)*
co-operative *(adj)*
comfortable *(adj)*
computer *(n)*
confident *(adj)*
construction *(n)*
employ *(v)*

employee *(n)*
employer *(n)*
employment *(n)*
explanation *(n)*
factory *(n)*
farm *(n)*
farmer *(n)*
finance *(n)*
friendly *(adj)*
government *(n)*
hobby *(n)*
imaginative *(adj)*
independent *(adj)*
interest *(n)*
interview *(n/v)*
kind *(adj)*
leisure *(n)*
manager *(n)*

manual worker *(n)*
manufacturing *(n)*
office worker *(n)*
organized *(adj)*
patient *(adj)*
personality *(n)*
professional *(n)*
punctual *(adj)*
responsibility *(n)*
retail *(n)*
salary *(n)*
sea *(n)*
shop *(n)*
shop assistant *(n)*
smart *(adj)*
trainee *(n)*
transport *(n)*

Lesson 1: Listening

A 1:28 **Listen and point.**

Example: *bank*

B 1:29 **Listen and match the employment sectors and the photographs.**

Example: *She works in a bank. She's in finance.*

agriculture	
construction	
finance	*1*
government	
leisure	
manufacturing	
retail	
transport	

C 1:30 **Listen to part of a lecture about employment in the UK. Complete Table 1.**

Table 1: *UK employment by sector (Winter 2003)*

Sector	%
other	7
Total	100

Source: *Labour Market Trends, June 2004*

D **Look at the photographs of different types of workers.**

1 What do we call each type of worker?
🔘 **1:31** Listen and check.

2 🔘 **1:32** Listen to the next part of the talk. What does the speaker say about each type of job? Tick (✓) the correct column for **M**anager, **P**rofessional, **O**ffice worker or **M**anual **W**orker.

	M	P	O	MW
boring				
comfortable				
easy				
hard				
high salaries				
interesting				
long hours				
making things				
outside				
responsibility				
years of study				

3 What kind of worker do you want to be? Why?

E **Look at Table 2.**

1 Predict the numbers and percentages.

2 🔘 **1:33** Listen to the last part of the talk.

Work in pairs to complete the table.

Student 1: Write the numbers.
Student 2: Write the percentages.

Exchange information.

3 Complete the key of Figure 1. Use information from Table 2.

Table 2: *US employment by type of worker (Aug 2010)*

	millions	%
manual workers		
office workers		
professionals		
managers		
	120	100%

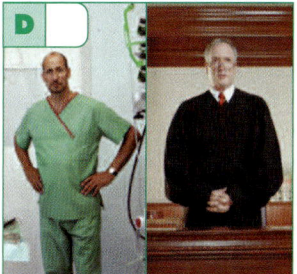

Skills Check

Transferring information to a table

Lecturers often give numbers and percentages.
Record this information in a table.
Leave spaces for information that you miss.
Example:

	millions	%
manual workers		42
office workers	35	

Check your figures with other students after the lecture.

What is the number for manual workers?

What is the percentage for office workers?

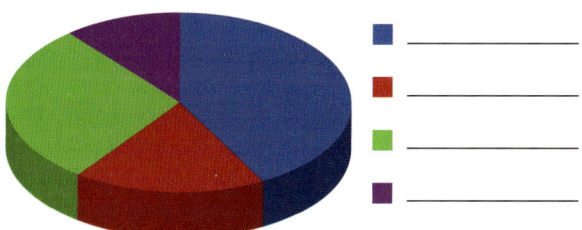

Figure 1: *US employment by type of worker (Aug 2010)*

A Look at the photographs.

1 Name the employment sectors.
Example: *1 agriculture*

2 Name some jobs in each sector.
Example: *1 farmer, farm worker, fruit picker*

3 Talk about employment sectors and jobs.
Examples:
I'd like to work in agriculture.
I'd like to be a farmer.

B Look at the flow chart. It gives advice on career planning.

1 🔘 **1:35** Listen to Paul and Jane. Which sector is good for Paul?

2 Make three questions from the flow chart. Ask and answer in pairs. Give true answers.

3 Which sector is good for you? Do you agree with the results of the flow chart?

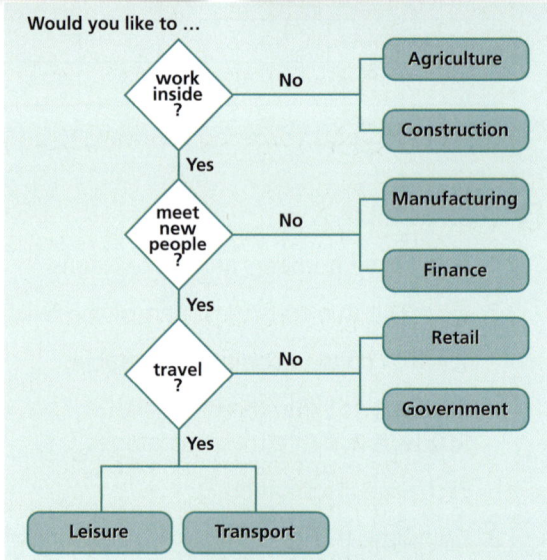

Would you like to ...

- work inside? — No → Agriculture / Construction
- meet new people? — No → Manufacturing / Finance
- travel? — No → Retail / Government
- Yes → Leisure / Transport

Pronunciation Check

Saying the infinitive

The infinitive is *to* + verb.
We usually pronounce *to* /tə/.
Examples:
I'd like to work in a bank.
I'm going to study Biology.

🔘 **1:34** Listen and repeat the sentences.

C 🔊 **1:36 Listen to the introduction to a talk at the training day.
What is the trainer going to talk about? Tick (✓) one subject.**

1 choosing a career ☐
2 starting your first job ☐
3 writing your resume ☐
4 preparing your presentation ☐

D 🔊 **1:37 Listen to the next part of the talk.**

1 What can you talk about in your presentation?
Number the areas that the trainer mentions.

achievements	☐
hobbies	☐
background	☐
interests	☐
career plans	☐
personality	☐
education	☐

Today
The Bristol Suite

Training Day from Educorp
Trainer: Angela Jones

From job interview ...
to career

9.00–10.00: Session 1
10.30–11.45: Session 2
12.00–1.30: Session 3
2.30–4.00: Session 4

2 What examples does she give for each area? Discuss in pairs.

E **Look at some sentences from a presentation.**

1 Which section of the presentation does each sentence come from?

2 Mark the main stressed words in each sentence.
🔊 **1:38** Listen and check.

3 Work in pairs. Tell your partner two things about yourself for
each area in Exercise D.

I have a certificate in First Aid.	3
I have two brothers and one sister.	☐
I passed the secondary certificate with 83%.	☐
I want to work in the leisure industry.	☐
I was head girl at my secondary school.	☐
I went to secondary school in Rome.	☐
I'd like to be a manager.	☐
I'm from Recife in northern Brazil.	☐

F **You are going to have a job interview.**

1 Prepare your presentation.

2 Give your presentation in groups.

Skills Check

Giving a presentation in
an interview

• You often have to give a
  presentation at job interviews.
  • Make notes.
  • Write out the presentation.
  • Practise it several times.
  • Record it and play it back.
  • Ask your friends for comments.

Lesson 3: Vocabulary and Pronunciation

  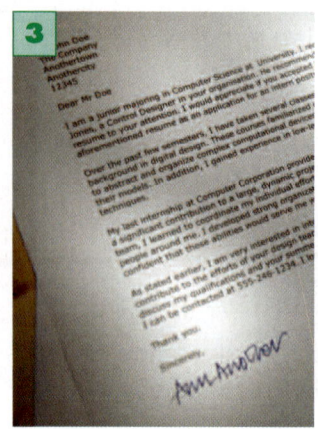 

A Look at the photographs above. They show the stages of getting a job.

1 Match the items in the box with the photographs.

> a job advertisement   a resume   an application letter   a job interview

2 🔊 **1:39** Listen to the phrases in the box. Where is the main stress in each word?

B Look at the conversations below.

1 Complete each conversation. Write one word in each space.

2 🔊 **1:40** Listen and check.

3 Role-play the conversations in pairs.

1

A: _____ you see this job advertisement?

B: No, I _____. What's it for?

A: Supastore _____ looking for a Trainee Manager.

B: _____ you going to apply?

A: Yes, I _____ so.

2

A: _____ you help me with my job application?

B: Sure. What _____ the problem?

A: They _____ my resume and a covering letter. What do I _____ in the letter?

B: _____ them about yourself, then tell them the reasons that you _____ applying for the job.

3

C: Thank you for coming _____ the interview.

A: Thank you _____ inviting me.

C: Let's start _____ some background information.

A: Certainly.

C: Tell me _____ yourself …

4

C: This is the manager _____ Supastore. We met yesterday _____ the interview.

A: Oh, yes. Hello.

C: Hi. We would like to offer you the job _____ Trainee Manager.

A: That's wonderful.

C: We want you to start _____ the Purchasing Department.

A: Yes, _____ course.

OBJECTIVES
• develop vocabulary related to job interviews and life skills
• stress within words – with change of part of speech

C **Make phrases using the verbs and nouns below.**

1	see	a job
2	apply for	a job advertisment
3	write	a presentation
4	prepare	a resume
5	have	a salary
6	talk about it	an interview
7	earn	long hours
8	work	yourself

Pronunciation Check

Stress within words

Stress sometimes moves when you change the part of speech.

Examples:

'advertise (v)   ad'vertisement (n)

pre'sent (v)   presen'tation (n)

Always check the stress of a new form of a word.

D **Look at the words in the table.**

1 Complete the table with the missing words. (Sometimes there is no missing word.) Mark the stress on each word.

2 🔘 **1:41** Listen and check your answers.

verb	noun	noun (person)	adjective
	application		
		employer /	un / employed
	interview	/	
qualify			
		trainer /	

E **Employers want people with life skills. What life skills do you have now?**

1 Tick (✓) the true sentences. Be honest!

2 Read the key and find out your life skills.

At university	
a. I always get to lectures on time.	
b. I always do my assignments on time.	
c. I always look clean and tidy.	
d. I work well in groups.	
e. I work well on my own.	
At home	
f. I look after younger brothers or sisters.	
g. I make up stories for my brothers or sisters.	
h. I care for an older relative.	
In your social life	
i. I have a lot of friends.	
j. I am the captain of a team.	

Key

Here are your life skills. You are:

a. punctual
b. organized
c. smart
d. co-operative
e. independent
f. kind
g. imaginative
h. patient
i. friendly
j. confident

Lesson 4: Reading

A Look at the text opposite. Read the heading and the introduction.

What is the article going to be about?

1 The reasons for getting a job.

2 The reasons for leaving school.

3 The reasons for continuing with your education.

B Study the figures opposite and complete the tables below.

Table 1: *Figure 1*

1 What does a person with a degree earn at 19?	
2 What does a person with a degree earn at 30?	
3 What about a person with secondary qualifications?	
4 What about a person with no qualifications?	
5 What happens to a person with a degree at age 22?	

Table 2: *Figure 2*

6 What percentage of graduates are unemployed?	
7 What about people with secondary qualifications?	
8 What about people without qualifications?	

C What are the reasons for going on to higher education?

1 What do the figures show?

2 Read the text and check your answers.

3 What other reasons are in the text?

D Look at the highlighted sentences in the text.

1 What is the *joining word* in each sentence?

2 What are the *subjects* and *verbs*?

E Guess the meaning of these words and phrases from context.

1	reasons	continue
2	promoted	education after school
3	go on	explanations
4	well-paid	get good money for a job
5	earn	get money or a salary for a job
6	unemployed	get a better job
7	higher education	without a job

What is the point of going on?

Do you ever say to yourself: *'I don't want to study any more? I'm going to leave school (or university) and get a job.'* In this article, we look at two good reasons to continue and get good qualifications.

In many countries, research
5 shows that higher education is very important for your future. Firstly, you earn more money because you have good qualifications
10 (see Figure 1). People with no qualifications do not get good jobs because most managers want qualified people. Well-paid jobs are
15 usually better jobs too, because they are more interesting. In addition, unqualified people have jobs, but they do not often have a
20 career. Well-qualified people usually start a career after university. They start at one level and they get promoted every three or four years.
25 You need to make a career plan. Ask yourself: *What employment sector am I going to work in? Where would I like to be in two*
30 *years, five years, ten years?*

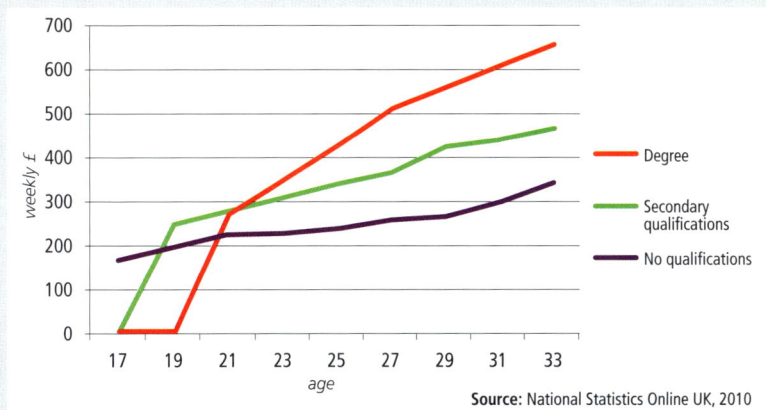

Figure 1: *Qualifications and earnings*

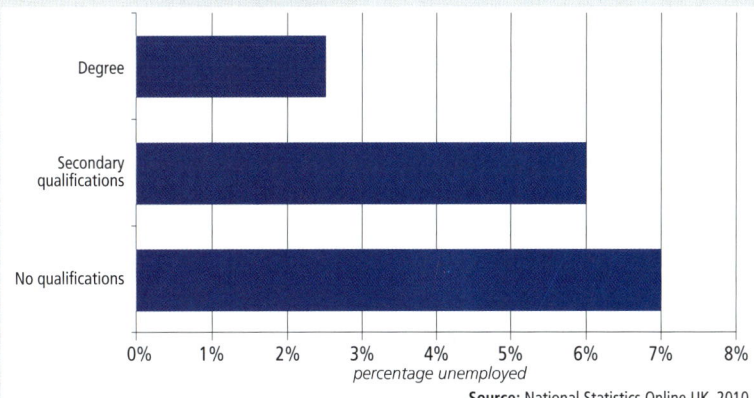

Figure 2: *Qualifications and unemployment rate*

Secondly, you may lose your job and you may become unemployed. However, well-qualified people are not that common, so a person with qualifications can usually get
35 another job quickly (see Figure 2). A well-qualified person can continue his or her career with a different company.

The message is clear. Go on to higher education, get good qualifications, and you
40 will soon have money for clothes and CDs *and* an interesting, well-paid job. And don't forget to make a career plan.

Lesson 5: Writing and Grammar

A Study the words below.

1 What do they all have in common?

2 Write the words with the correct spelling.

a. aply _____

b. asignment _____

c. asistant _____

d. comunicate _____

e. diferent _____

f. milion _____

g. ofer _____

h. ofice _____

i. profesional _____

B Using *a* or *an*.

1 Write *a* or *an* in front of each noun or noun phrase.

a. _____ job

b. _____ bank

c. _____ manager

d. _____ advertisement

e. _____ e-mail

f. _____ office

g. _____ international bank

h. _____ English company

i. _____ average salary

j. _____ European

k. _____ university

l. _____ UN job

m. _____ hour

n. _____ Xbox

2 Work out the rule.

C What are your job skills now?

1 Look back at Lesson 3. Then write six sentences. Use different patterns.

2 Add an example for each point.
Example:
I am an organized person. I always do my assignments on time.

Skills Check 1

Doubled letters

Some English words have doubled consonants. There is no rule for these words. The double consonant has the same sound as the single consonant.
Examples:
apple, yellow, coffee

Skills Check 2

Using *a* or *an*

There are three main rules.

Rule 1
We use *a/an* with nouns.
Examples:
a job, ***an*** *application*

Rule 2
We put *a/an* in front of an adjective + noun phrase.
Examples:
a good interview, ***an*** *interesting job*

Rule 3
We use *a* if the next word begins with a **consonant sound**.
We use *an* if the next word begins with a **vowel sound**.
Examples:
a useful job, ***an*** *honest person*

Skills Check 3

Statement + example

In essays and business letters, we often make a statement, then give a example. The example helps people to understand or believe the statement.
Example:

statement	I am a very confident person.
example	I am captain of my local football team.

When you make a statement, try to give an example.

OBJECTIVES
- spell with doubled consonants
- use statement + example
- use the indefinite article
- grammar: *going to* future

D **Look at Table 1.**

1 When do we use this pattern?
Tick (✓) one or more use.

- to introduce a lecture ☐
- to talk about past events ☐
- to talk about present actions ☐
- to talk about future plans ☐

2 What are you going to do …
- in this lesson?
- in the next unit?
- after this course?

E **Look at Table 2. Compare it with Table 1.**

1 How do we make *yes/no* questions with this pattern?

2 How do we make answers? Guess!

F **Look at Table 3. Compare it with Table 2.**

1 Complete each question.

2 How do we make *wh~* questions with this pattern?

3 Work in pairs. Ask about your partner's plans for the future. Use *yes/no* and *wh~* questions.

4 Write about your partner's plans for the future.

G **Look at Table 4.**

1 Make two sentences from the table with the same meaning.

2 Write a *yes/no* question for each kind of sentence.

3 Check your questions with Table 5.

4 How can you answer each question?

5 Make two sentences with the subject *she*.

6 Make two questions with the subject *he*.

Table 1: going to *statements*

S	V1	V2	Other
I	am	to talk	about Africa today.
He	is	to study	in the USA next year.
She	is	going	to do	Mathematics.
We	are	to learn	to find areas this lesson.
They	are	to leave	school in July.

Table 2: yes/no *questions*

V1	S	V1	V2	Other
Are	you		to talk	about Mexico today?
Is	he		to study	in Canada next year?
Is	she	going	to do	Geography at university?
Are	we		to learn	how to write letters in this lesson?
Are	they		to start	primary school next month?

Table 3: wh~ *questions*

Q word	V1	S	V1	V2	Other
_____	are	you		to talk	about?
_____	is	he		to study	next year?
_____	is	she	going	to start	school?
_____	are	we		to get	to college?
_____	are	they		to leave	next year?

Table 4: want *vs* would like

Subject	Verb	Infinitive	Other
I	want	to work	in a hotel.
	would	like		

Table 5: *statements/questions*

Verb	Subject	Verb	Infinitive	Other	
Do	you	want	to work	in a hotel	?
Would		like			

Lesson 6: Writing and Grammar

A **Read the sentences below. They all come from an application letter.**
Use a clause from the box to complete each sentence.

I saw your advertisement for a trainee manager in the *Daily News* this morning.

1 I am writing to you because …

2 My name is Francesca Mori. I am 21 and …

3 I am doing a degree in Psychology. I am going to finish my course in two weeks and …

4 I am going to stay in Milton so …

5 I would like to work in the retail industry because …

6 During my degree course, I worked as a shop assistant at the weekends, so …

Skills Check

Using *because* and *so*

These two words are similar. But notice the order of the information in each case.

statement	joining word	reason
I want to be a teacher	because	I like children.

statement	joining word	reason
I like children	so	I want to be a teacher.

I am studying at Milton University.	I want a job in the city.
I love working in shops.	I want to start work immediately.
I understand retail work.	I would like to apply for the job.

B **Read the sentences below. They come from the same application letter.**
Match each statement with an example.

#		
1	I am a punctual person.	At home, I often look after my little brother. He is four.
2	I love meeting people.	I am never late for lectures or meetings.
3	I am patient.	I do not ask for help on assignments. I do everything myself.
4	I am independent.	I go to many clubs at university.
5	I am an organized person.	I often do the shopping for my family and I cook many meals.
6	I am an imaginative person.	I write stories and I paint pictures.

C **How can you start and end a business letter? Choose one starting phrase and one ending phrase.**

Starting
1 Good morning,
2 Hello. How are you?
3 Hi,
4 Sir,
5 Dear Mr or Mrs,
6 Dear Sir or Madam,

Ending
1 Best wishes,
2 Goodbye,
3 Yours faithfully,
4 Lots of love,
5 See you later,
6 Yours,

D Read the sentences. Circle the correct word or phrase in each case.

1	I would	**like** / liking	a well-paid job.
2	I don't	would like / want	to work inside.
3	He	woulds / would	like to leave school.
4	She wants	to work / work	for the government.
5	Do you	want / would like	to go on to college?
6	I am going	finish / to finish	my course in July.
7	I want to work for the government	so / because	I want to help my country.
8	What	you going / are you going	to do after university?

E You want to apply for a job. You are going to write an application letter.

1 Make some notes.

Where did you see the advertisement?	
What is the job?	
What is your name?	
What is your age?	
What is your present situation?	
What are you studying?	
When can you start the job?	
Why do you want this job?	
Why are you good for this job?	

2 Write the application letter. Use patterns from Exercises A, B and C on the opposite page.

Grade your progress (1 = poor to 5 = very good)

At the end of Unit 3, I can:

☐ listen and transfer information into a table

☐ give a presentation for a job interview

☐ use stress appropriately within word families

☐ use link words to aid text comprehension

☐ use statement + examples appropriately

☐ use the grammar of the unit accurately

Transfer

Imagine you are going for a job interview and have to discuss the reasons for your choice of college or university study. Think about what you would say and practise with a friend.

Reflect

Think about the skills of listening, speaking and reading you have been studying in Unit 3. How do you feel the grammar in Lessons 5 and 6 has helped you with these skills?

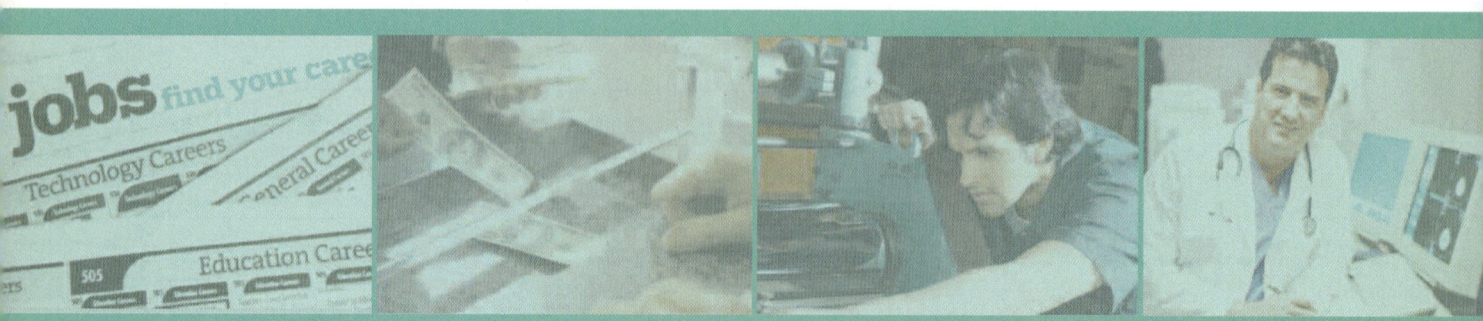

Unit 4
Science and Nature

Key vocabulary

affect *(v)*
altitude *(n)*
autumn *(n)*
bear *(n)*
beautiful *(adj)*
boring *(adj)*
climate *(n)*
cloudy *(adj)*
cold *(adj)*
dangerous *(adj)*
difficult *(adj)*
dog *(n)*
dry *(adj)*
effect *(n)*
fast *(adj)*

foggy *(n)*
fur *(n)*
high *(adj)*
hot *(adj)*
humid *(adj)*
leg *(n)*
lightning *(n)*
lips *(n)*
low *(adj)*
mild *(adj)*
modern *(adj)*
neck *(n)*
nose *(n)*
paw *(n)*
protected *(adj)*

rain *(v)*
region *(n)*
season *(n)*
skin *(n)*
spring *(n)*
storm *(n)*
summer *(n)*
sunny *(adj)*
temperature *(n)*
tropical *(adj)*
valley *(n)*
warm *(adj)*
weight *(n)*
wet *(adj)*
winter *(n)*

Unit 4 Science and Nature

Lesson 1: Listening

A 🔊 **1:42 Listen. Which photograph(s) can you see each item in?**

Example: *trees – Photographs 1, 2 and 3*

B 🔊 **1:43 Listen to four descriptions by students.**

1 Which photograph is the speaker describing?

2 Write the name for the season under each picture.

C 🔊 **1:44 Listen to a short talk about seasons. Complete the table. Guess the spelling of each place name.**

Place	Number of seasons	Other information

Skills Check

Guessing spelling

- Most **consonant sounds** in English only have **one** common **spelling**.
  Examples:
  /b/, /d/, /g/, /h/, /l/, /m/, /n/, /p/, /r/, /t/, /w/
- Most **vowel sounds** in English can have **many spellings**. However, there are some common sound/letter(s) combinations.

Sound	Common spelling	Example
/ɒ/	o	Bosnia
/æ/	a	Canada
/e/	e	Venezuela
/ɪ/	i	India
/ɔː/	or	Portugal
/ɑː/	ar	Arctic
/ɜː/	er	Germany
	ur	Turkey

OBJECTIVES
- predict with *and, but, or, because*
- complete the key to a map
- guess spelling
- learn about climate types

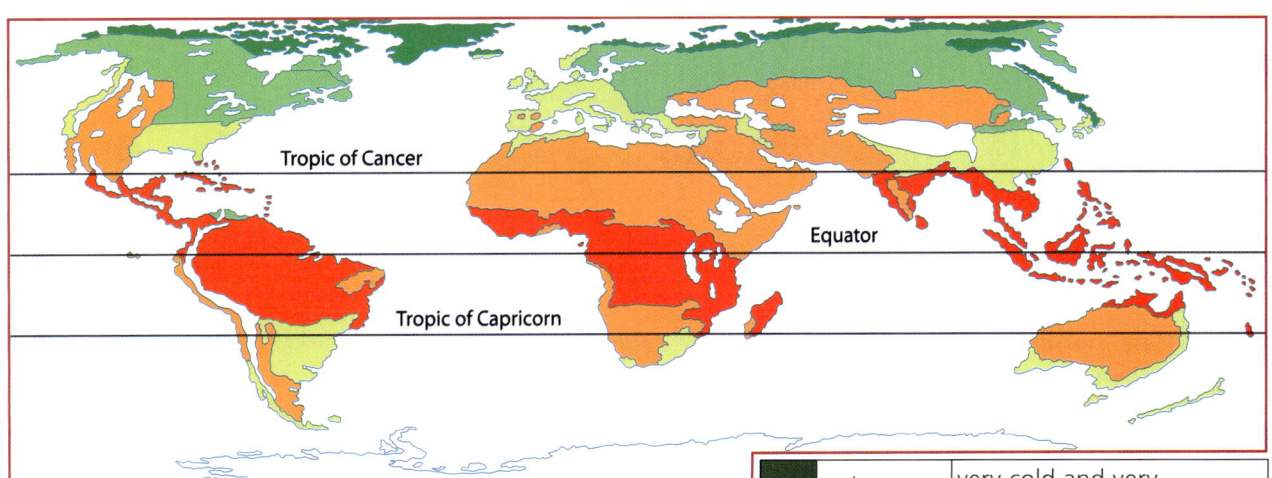

![dark green]	polar	very cold and very _____
![green]		cold and _____
![yellow]		warm and humid
![orange]		hot in daytime, but _____ at night
![red]		hot and _____
![white]		altitude affects _____

D Look at the place names in the box.

1 Is each place a continent, a country or a region?

> Africa   Antarctica   Asia   Australia   China   Europe
> The Middle East   Greenland   India   North America
> Oceania   Russia   South America   The USA

2 Find all the places on the map.

E 🔘 1:45 **Listen to the introduction to a lecture about climate.**

Use the phrases in the box to make a definition of *climate*.

> in a region   it is   of time   over a long period
> the normal pattern   of weather

F 🔘 1:46 **Listen to the main part of the lecture. Look at the key above.**

1 Complete the information about each climate type. Guess the spelling.

2 What is the climate type for your country?

G 🔘 1:47 **Listen to the summary. Number the next piece of information in each case.**

it is still cold. ☐

information about climate types. ☐ *1*

not cold. ☐

not very much rain. ☐

the land is very high. ☐

the South Pole. ☐

the Tropic of Capricorn. ☐

very cold at night. ☐

🔘 1:48 **Listen and check.**

Lesson 2: Speaking

An Inuit woman

An Inuit igloo

An Inuit dog sled

Masai men with spears

Masai mud huts

A Masai man with his cows

A **Look at the photographs above.**

Discuss these questions. Which region:

1 is cold / hot / dry / sunny / cloudy / humid?

2 is high above sea level?

3 has a lot of snow / rain?

4 is hard to live in?

5 is interesting to visit?

B 🔵 **1:49 Listen to a tutor. Look at the handout on the right.**

1 What **extra** information is in the handout?

2 Which highlighted word in the text means:

   a. the normal pattern of weather in a region over a long period of time

   b. a meeting with a tutor to discuss ideas about a topic

   c. a university department for a subject or group of subjects.

   d. an area with humans, plants, animals, etc.

   e. change

   f. mountains, rivers, deserts, etc.

   g. plants, animals, insects

Human Geography Faculty

Tutorial 2:
Date: Wednesday 15th
Time: 3.00
Room: B7

Topic: *How do humans adapt to their environment?*

Before the tutorial, do some research on:
the Inuit in Northern Canada
or
the Masai in East Africa.

Find out about their region.
In particular, research:
• the geography of the region
• the climate
• other living things in the region

C 🔘 **1:50 Listen to part of the tutorial. Make notes about the Inuit in the table on the right.**

D **Read the parts of the tutorial below.**

1 Complete the sentences.

2 Check with the Skills Check.

3 Practise the parts in pairs.

S1: Right. So what can you _tell us about_ the Inuit?
S2: OK, well, first, geography.

S1: Some of the land is an ice sheet.
S2: Sorry. What is _____?
S1: It's a large area of ice on top of the sea.

S2: OK. Go _____.
S1: Right. The Inuit live in a polar climate so it is very cold.

S1: Oh, I forgot _____. The temperature in winter sometimes goes down to minus 75.
S2: Sorry. What did _____?
S1: Minus 75.

S1: So how do they adapt to their environment?
S2: Well, there _____. Firstly, they have very thick clothes. Secondly …

S1: Anything _____?
S2: Um. Yes, they use the dogs from the region.

E **Research information.**

1 Read the information about the geography of the Masai region.

2 Work in groups. Read the information your teacher gives you about climate or other living things.

F **Role-play a tutorial about the Masai.**

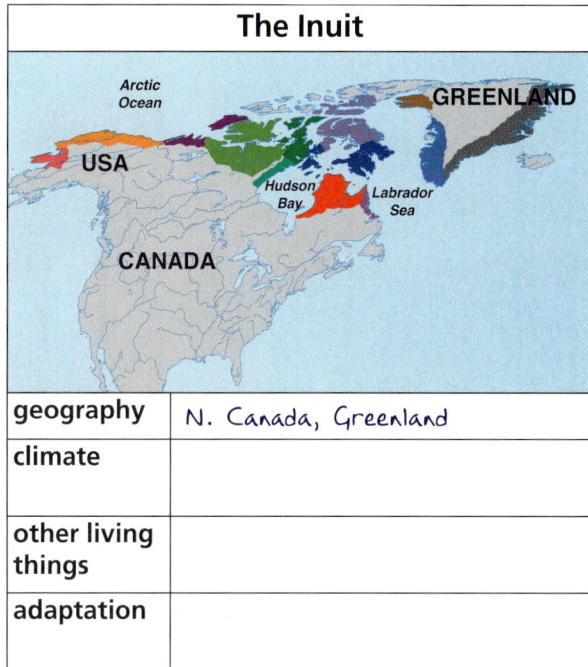

The Inuit

geography	N. Canada, Greenland
climate	
other living things	
adaptation	

Skills Check

Taking part in a tutorial

Learn important phrases in tutorials.

From the speaker	*There are (two) main (ways)* *Firstly / Secondly* *Oh, I forgot to say.*
From the listeners	*What can you tell us about …* *What is / are …?* *What did you say?* *Go on.* *Anything else?*

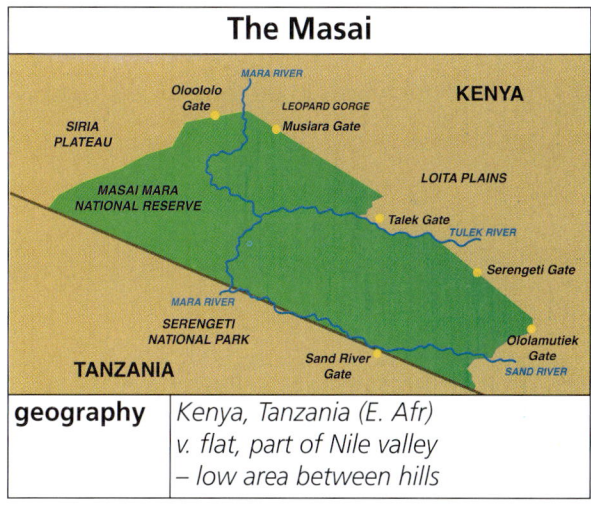

The Masai

geography	*Kenya, Tanzania (E. Afr)* *v. flat, part of Nile valley* *– low area between hills*

Lesson 3: Vocabulary and Pronunciation

Ⓐ Ask and answer in pairs.

1 What's the weather like today?

2 What was the weather like last weekend?

3 What will the weather be like tomorrow?

Ⓑ Look at the words in the box on the right.

1 Mark each word (**adj**)ective or (**v**)erb.

2 Ask about the weather in the photographs above. Use words from the box.

   Example: *What's the weather like in photograph 1?*
   It's foggy.

Ⓒ Look at the questions in Exercise A above.

Underline the verb in each question. Circle the preposition.

cloudy	cold	dry	foggy	hot	raining
snowing	stormy	sunny	wet	windy	

OBJECTIVES
• develop vocabulary related to weather
• say *the*
• use the preposition *like*
• start a conversation about the weather

D **Look at the conversation on the right.**

1 🔘 **1:51** Listen. Follow the conversation in the pictures.

2 🔘 **1:52** Listen and repeat.

3 Practise the conversation in pairs.

4 Have another conversation. Change some of the words.

E 🔘 **1:53** **Listen to some conversations. Answer the questions about each conversation.**

1 What's the weather forecast for the weekend?

2 What's the average summer temperature in London?

3 What's the climate like in Bulent's country?

4 Which season is it?

Pronunciation Check

Saying *the*

We pronounce the letter *e* in *the* in two ways:

1 **before a consonant letter** /ðə/
   Examples: the day; the night.

2 **before a vowel letter** /ðiː/
   Examples: the answer, the elephants

Mark each *the* 1 or 2 in these sentences.
What's the forecast for the weekend? __
What's the average temperature in the summer? __
What about in the autumn? __
It's dark at five in the evening now. __

🔘 **1:54** Listen and check.
Practise saying the sentences.

Skills Check

Starting a conversation

We often talk about the weather at the start of a conversation.
Examples:
It's nice today.
Is it raining outside?
What a lovely day!

🔘 **1:55** Listen to the start of some conversations.
Practise in pairs.

Lesson 4: Reading

Ⓐ Look at the text opposite. Read the heading and the introduction.

What will the text talk about? Number the correct items below in the correct order. Look quickly at the text and check.

animal adaptation in general	☐
climate change	☐
clothes	☐
giraffes	☐
houses	☐
polar bears	☐

Skills Check

Using an introduction

Many texts begin with an introduction. The introduction is the first paragraph. Read the introduction carefully. It answers two questions.

1 What information will be in this text?

2 What order will the information be in?

Ⓑ Look at the photographs on the right.

What do you know about polar bears?
What about giraffes?

Ⓒ Read the second paragraph. Underline the word which means:

1	live (v), not die	survive
2	colours or patterns to hide in an environment	
3	get to something high	
4	kept from danger	
5	a hard covering	
6	living, staying alive	

polar bears

giraffes

Ⓓ Work in pairs.

Student 1: Read about **polar bears**.
Student 2: Read about **giraffes**.

1 Find these parts of the body in the photographs. Make notes about adaptations.

fur	leg	lips	neck	nose	paw	skin

2 Tell your partner about your animal.

elephants

turtles

Ⓔ Read the final paragraph.

Why is climate change a problem for animals?

Ⓕ Look at the highlighted words in the text.

1 What part of speech are they?

2 Find more examples of these kinds of words in the text.

Adapting to the environment

How do animals live in different regions of the world? Humans and other living things adapt to their environment. Humans adapt their behaviour. They build warm houses or cool houses. They wear warm clothes or cool clothes. Animals adapt in a different way. Over thousands of years, animals adapt their bodies to their environment. In this article, we look first at animal adaptation in general. Then we see the adaptations of two particular animals – the polar bear and the giraffe. Finally, we consider the effects of climate change. Can animals adapt?

Animals adapt to survive in an environment. Animals survive for many reasons. Some animals are stronger than other animals. Some animals are faster. Some animals have better camouflage, so other animals can't see them. Some animals are taller so they can reach fruit or leaves. Some animals are more protected. For example, the elephant has a thick skin, and the turtle has a shell. Better adapted animals live. Adaptation is the key to survival.

Polar bears live in a region of ice and snow. They have white fur so it is difficult to see them in their environment. The fur is thick so they stay warm. They have big paws. The paws spread their weight so they can walk on the snow. Polar bears eat fish so they have to be good swimmers. Their big paws help them swim. They can close their noses under the water.

Giraffes live in a region of grassland and high trees. They have brown and yellow skin so it is difficult to see them in their environment. They have long thin legs so they stay cool. They have long necks so they can eat leaves from the high trees. The trees have thorns, but giraffes have thick lips so they do not get hurt. Their long necks also help them to see lions and leopards in the distance.

Many scientists say that the climate is changing. Can humans and animals adapt to climate change? Humans can adapt because they can change their behaviour. They can wear thicker clothes or make their houses cooler. Animals can adapt too, but it takes thousands of years. Animals cannot change their bodies in twenty or fifty years.

Lesson 5: Writing and Grammar

A **Study the words in the box.**

1 Which ones are adjectives?

2 What part of speech are the other words?

better	consider	cooler	danger
faster	stronger	summer	winter

B **Study the words below. They are all from the listening and the reading in this unit.**

1 Write the comparative form of each adjective. Be careful with spelling!

2 Read the Skills Checks and check your answers.

a.	fast	faster
b.	tall	
c.	thick	
d.	cool	
e.	cloudy	
f.	big	
g.	protected	
h.	dangerous	
i.	good	
j.	bad	

C **Look at Table 1 below.**

Write four sentences. Compare the two towns.

Example: *The Masai town is higher than the Innuit town.*

Skills Check 1

Comparative adjectives (1)

We make one-syllable adjectives into comparatives with ~er.

Examples:

*Spring is warm**er** than winter.*

*Giraffes have long**er** necks than bears.*

With most short adjectives, we just add ~(e)r. But we sometimes change the spelling before adding ~er.

Examples:

cold	colder;	large	larger
dry	drier;	sunny	sunnier
hot	hotter;	big	bigger

Skills Check 2

Comparative adjectives (2)

With long adjectives, we put *more* in front of the adjective.

Examples:

humid	more humid
interesting	more interesting

Skills Check 3

Comparative adjectives (3)

With a small number of adjectives, we use a different word for the comparative.

Examples:

good	better
bad	worse

Table 1: *Comparison of Inuit town and Masai town*

	Inuit town*	Masai town**
Height (above sea level)	29 m	2,000 m
Ave. temperature	-4°C	28°C
Ave. rainfall p.a.	263 mm	1,000 mm
Ave. sunshine per day	5.1 hours	8 hours

*Ilulissat   **Kichwas Tembo

D Look at Tables 2 and 3.

1 What do we use comparative adjectives for? Tick (✓) one use:

- to talk about one thing ☐   • to compare many things ☐
- to compare two things ☐

2 Complete the tables.

3 Make the comparative statements into *yes/no* questions.

4 Complete these sentences with something true.

a. My country is warmer than …

b. My town or city is bigger than …

c. I am older than …

d. The climate in my country was … in the past.

e. The weather today is … yesterday.

f. English is … Maths.

g. My friend is … me.

h. Reading / playing sport.

i. Nile / Amazon

j. Africa / Asia

5 Make the sentences in question 4 into questions. Ask your partner.

Table 2: *Comparatives with short adjectives*

Greenland	_____	colder	_____	Kenya.
Giraffes	_____	faster	_____	elephants.

Table 3: *Comparatives with longer adjectives*

Kenya	_____		humid	_____	Greenland.
Elephants	_____	_____	protected	_____	giraffes.

E Look at Table 4.

1 What is the main difference between this table and Tables 2 and 3? Why don't we finish the sentence?

2 What is the second item in these sentences?

a. Some people are happier.

b. Some plants are nicer to eat.

c. Some dogs are more dangerous.

d. There are two main differences between me and my friend. I am taller and thinner.

e. There are many differences between humans and animals. Humans are more intelligent …

f. … but animals are more adapted to their environment.

Table 4: *Comparatives with no second item*

Some animals	are		faster.	(than other animals).
		more	protected.	

Lesson 6: Writing and Grammar

A **Study the sentences opposite.**

1 Underline the verb(s) in each sentence.

2 Which adverb is in the first two sentences?

3 Which adverb is in the third and fourth sentences?

4 Tick (✓) the correct rule for using the words *only* and *also*?

   a. They go before *be* and after other verbs. ☐

   b. They go after all verbs. ☐

   c. They go after *be* and before other verbs. ☐

   d. They go before all verbs. ☐

5 Read the Skills Check and check your answers.

B **Rewrite the sentences with *only* in the correct place.**

1 Jungles are in tropical climates.
   Jungles are only in tropical climates.

2 In some regions, it rains in winter.

3 Tigers live in Asia.

4 There are about 1,500 tigers in India.

5 We find Giant Pandas in China.

6 Pandas eat the leaves of one plant.

7 The temperature is 2°C today.

8 There are a few rivers in Australia.

C **Read each sentence. Then complete the second sentence with the word *also*.**

1 Some snakes are dangerous. Some insects …
   are also dangerous.

2 It rains in autumn. It …

3 We studied animals. We …

4 The climate is hot. It …

5 The animals live in Europe. They …

6 It was cloudy yesterday. It …

7 Giraffes have long legs. They …

8 The paws of polar bears help them to walk on snow. They …

There are only a few bushes in the area.

Some parts of the world only have two seasons.

The region is cold and it is also humid.

Baga has two seasons and Nazca also has two seasons.

Skills Check

Using *only* and *also*

The words *only* and *also* are adverbs. They tell us something extra about the information in the sentence.

only = the writer thinks the object/ complement is:

   a small number or amount.

or   **in a small group**

also = the writer thinks the object/ complement is:

   the same or similar.

Examples:

*He is **only** five. (= very young)*

*She is **also** five. (= the same age as her)*

*She **only** has one brother. (= people have more)*

*He **also** has one brother. (= the same as him)*

The words go:

1 **after** the verb **be**

2 **before** other **verbs**

tiger

panda

snake

D **Look at the information about African elephants and Asian elephants.
Then circle the correct word or phrase in each sentence below.**

1	There	is / ~~are~~	two main kinds of elephant.
2	African elephants	live / are living	in tropical climates in central and south Africa.
3	Asian elephants	also live / live also	in tropical climates in India and south east Asia.
4	Both kinds of elephant are	grey. / grey colour.	
5	There	only are / are only	about 10,000 African elephants …
6	… and 30,000	of Asian elephants. / Asian elephants.	
7	African elephants are	more heavy / heavier	than Asian elephants.
8	They are also	taller. / more tall.	
9	Asian elephants have	the smoother / smoother	skins.
10	Their ears are	smaller. / small than.	

E **You are going to write a comparison of two kinds of bears.**

1 Study Table 1 on the right. Find some similarities and differences.

2 Write your text. Use some patterns from Exercise D above.

This essay is about polar bears and brown bears.

Table 1: *Polar bears and brown bears*

	polar bear	brown bear
location	Russia, Canada, Greenland	Russia, Canada, the USA
climate	polar	continental
number	c.30,000	c.130,000
colour	white fur	cream to black fur
weight	c.500 kg	c.300 kg
length	3 m	2.8 m
speed	30 kph	56 kph
danger to humans	high	low

At the end of Unit 4, I can:

- ☐ use linking words as signposts to aid listening comprehension

- ☐ take part in a tutorial role play

- ☐ use conversation starters appropriately

- ☐ use an introduction to predict the content of a written text

- ☐ use comparatives in written text

- ☐ use the grammar of the unit accurately

Transfer

Think about the weather where you live and whether you would prefer it to be different. If so, find a climate you would prefer and compare with your own. If not, find a climate that is worse, then think about why yours is better. Talk about it to a classmate.

Reflect

Think about the four topics you have studied so far. Which did you find most interesting and why?

Unit 5

The Physical World

Key vocabulary

above *(prep)*
ago *(adv)*
away from *(prep)*
behind *(prep)*
below *(prep)*
between *(prep)*
bottom *(adj)*
deep *(adj)*
depth *(n)*
the Earth *(n)*
east *(adj)*
far *(adj)*
hemisphere *(n)*
in front of *(prep)*
in the centre *(prep)*
in the corner *(prep)*

into *(prep)*
Jupiter *(n)*
left *(adv)*
length *(n)*
liquid *(n)*
Mars *(n)*
Mercury *(n)*
the Moon *(n)*
near *(adj)*
Neptune *(n)*
next to *(prep)*
north *(adj)*
old *(adj)*
out of *(prep)*
over *(prep)*
planet *(n)*

right *(adv)*
rock *(n)*
Saturn *(n)*
the Solar System *(n)*
solid *(n)*
south *(adj)*
the Sun *(n)*
top *(adj)*
towards *(prep)*
under *(prep)*
Uranus *(n)*
Venus *(n)*
west *(adj)*
wide *(adj)*
width *(n)*
young *(adj)*

Lesson 1: Listening

Figure 1: *The planets of the Solar System*

Ⓐ Look at Figure 1.

1 You are going to hear a lecture about the Earth and the Solar System. How will the lecturer pronounce the names of the planets?

2 💿 **2:1** Listen and check.

3 Which part of the Solar System is the speaker talking about? 💿 **2:2** Listen and point to the item in each case.

Example: *It's next to the Sun – Mercury*

4 💿 **2:3** Listen and complete each sentence with a name from Figure 1.

Example: *At the centre of the Solar System is ... the Sun.*

Ⓑ Look at Figure 2.

1 How will the lecturer pronounce each key word?

2 💿 **2:4** Listen and check.

3 Which part of the Earth's core is the speaker talking about? 💿 **2:5** Listen and point to the part in each case.

Example: *It's at the centre of the Earth. – The inner core*

4 💿 **2:6** Listen and complete each sentence with a word or phrase from Figure 2.

Example: *The top part of the Earth is called ... the crust.*

Ⓒ 💿 **2:7 Listen and write the answer.**

Example: *Which is the nearest planet to the Sun?*
Mercury

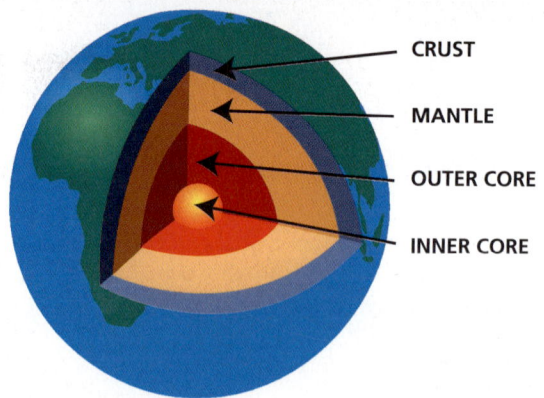

Figure 2: *The Earth's core*

CRUST
MANTLE
OUTER CORE
INNER CORE

Skills Check 1

Recognizing key words in a lecture

You must recognize names and key topic words in a lecture. Do some research before the lecture. Check the pronunciation of key words from the topic. You can also guess:

- the stressed syllable
  nouns and adjectives = usually 1st syllable
  verbs = usually 2nd syllable

- the pronunciation of key sounds
  Think of similar letter combinations.

Examples: *Mer*cury – *per*son
*Ju*piter – *June*

Skills Check 2

Superlative adjectives (1)

We make one-syllable adjectives into superlatives with ~*est*. We use *the*.

Examples:

The smallest planet in the Solar System is called Mercury.
The inner core is **the deepest** part of the Earth.

OBJECTIVES
- recognize key words
- understand prepositions of location and movement
- recognize superlatives
- use diagrams to record information

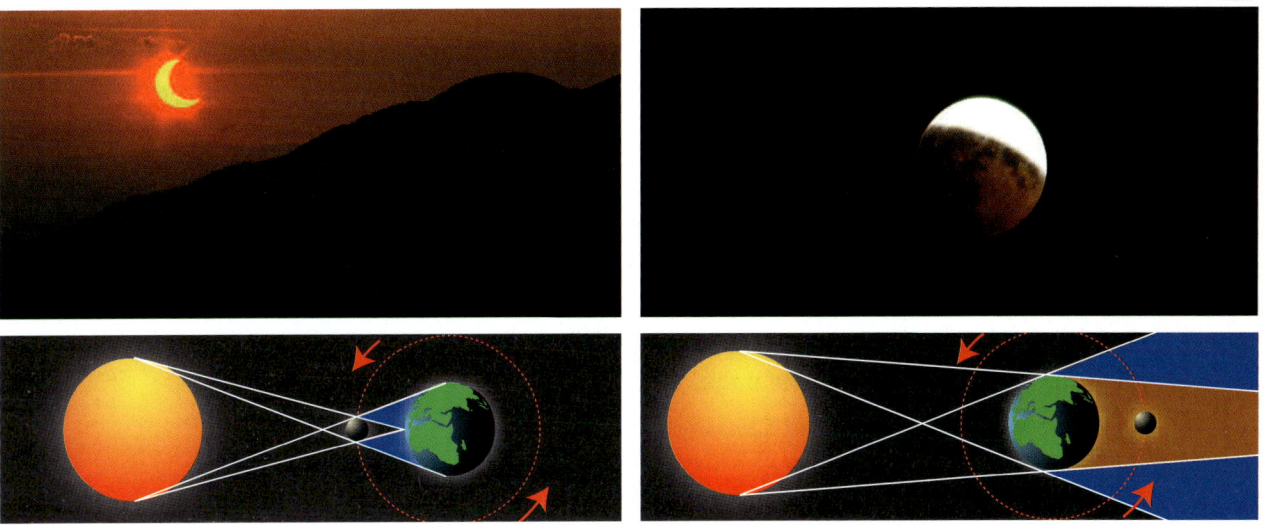

Figure 3　　　　　　　　　　　　　　　　**Figure 4**

D 🔊 **2:8 Listen to the introduction to the lecture.**

1 What is the lecturer going to talk about?

2 How can you spell the word?

E 🔊 **2:9 Listen to the first part of the lecture.**

1 When the lecturer stops, number the final word in the sentence.

completely. ☐	eclipse. ☐	moves. ☐	show? ☐
diagrams. ☐	left. ☐	part. ☐	Sun. ☐
Earth. ☐	Moon. ☐	photograph. ☐	years. ☐

2 🔊 **2:10** Listen again to this part and check.

F **Look at the second photograph and diagram.**

1 What is the lecturer going to say about them?

2 🔊 **2:11** Listen to the second part of the lecture and check your answers.

G **Work in pairs.**

1 🔊 **2:12** Listen to some sentences about Figures 3 and 4. Which figure is the speaker talking about in each case?

Example: *The diagram shows an eclipse of the Sun. – Figure 4.*

2 Close your books. Draw a diagram of an eclipse, then explain it to your partner.
Student 1: Draw an eclipse of the Sun.
Student 2: Draw an eclipse of the Moon.

Skills Check 3

Understanding prepositions

We often use **prepositions** to talk about:

1 location

2 movement

Examples:

*The Moon is **between** the Sun and the Earth.*

*The Moon goes **round** the Earth.*

Use diagrams to show position and movement when you are listening to a lecture.

Which prepositions of **place** (location) did you hear during the lecture? What about prepositions of **movement**?

Lesson 2: Speaking

A **Study Figure 1 opposite.**

  1 Name the continents. **Example:** *Number 1 is Asia.*

  2 Name some of the countries in each continent.
    Example: *Canada is in North America.*

B 🔊 **2:13 Listen to the start of a lecture. Complete the introduction on the right.**

C 🔊 **2:14 Listen to the main part of the lecture and look at Figures 2, 3 and 4 on the opposite page.**

  1 Write the date for each figure. Add names to the figure. Guess the spellings of the names.

  2 Check your answers in pairs.

D 🔊 **2:15 Listen to the last part and look again at Figure 4.**

  1 Label the continents. Show the movements of the continents with arrows.

  2 Check again in pairs.

E **You will listen to students in a group discussion.**

  1 Complete the conversations below with questions from the box. 🔊 **2:16** Listen and check your answers.

  2 Practise the conversations in pairs.

> Today, I'm going to talk to you about the history of the _____. I don't mean the _____ history. I mean the _____ history. Where were the continents million of years _____? According to scientists, they weren't in the same _____ as today. They were in _____ places, and they _____ very different, too.

S1: There was only one continent 250 million years ago.
S2: That's right. _____
S1: Pangea, I think. It means 'all lands'.

S1: _____
S2: It split into two parts.
S1: _____
S2: Yes, Laurasia and Gondwanaland.

S1: _____
S2: Well, there were seven continents, but they were in different places.
S1: _____
S2: Um, North America moved away from Europe and Asia and, ... er ... India moved towards Asia.

S1: _____
S2: Well, the continents are on the crust and the crust is above the mantle.
S1: Right. _____
S2: It's not solid. It's liquid.

> And what's important about the mantle?
>
> Can you remember the names?
>
> How can the continents move?
>
> What happened to Pangea 200 million years ago?
>
> What was it called?
>
> What was the world like 85 million years ago?
>
> What changed in the next 50 million years?

F **Discuss in groups.**
Close your books. How much information can you remember from this lesson?

OBJECTIVES
- talk about the past with a day or date
- talk about the past with a time period + *ago*
- talk about the past with *last* + time period

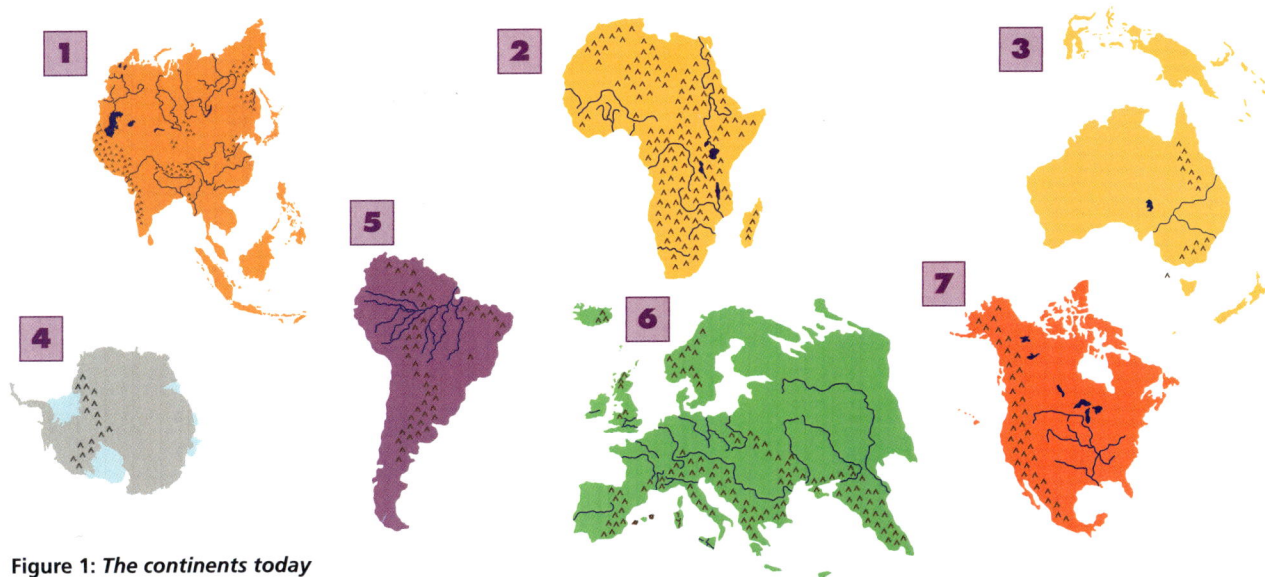

Figure 1: *The continents today*

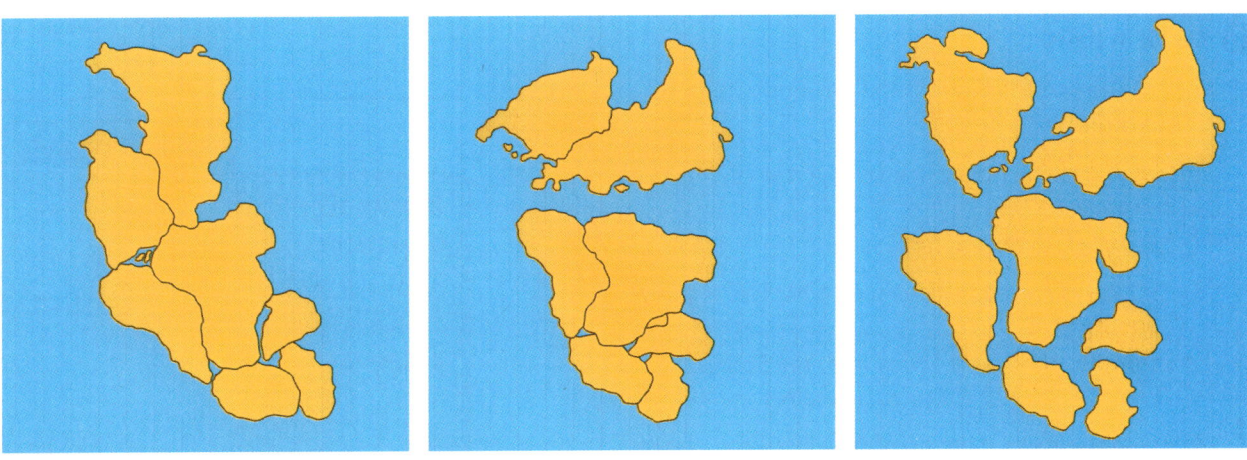

Figure 2 **Figure 3** **Figure 4**

Skills Check

Talking about the past

We can talk about the past:

1 with a day or a date   **2 with *last* + time period**   **3 with a time period + *ago***

Examples:

1 *We talked about the continents **yesterday**.*
   On 11th July, 2010, *there was a total eclipse of the Sun.*

2 *We looked at eclipses **last week**.*
   ***Last year**, I studied eclipses.*

3 *John Couch Adams discovered Neptune **one hundred and sixty-five years ago**.*
   ***Two hundred and thirty years ago**, William Herschel discovered Uranus.*

The time phrase can go at the **beginning** of the sentence, or the **end**.

Lesson 3: Vocabulary and Pronunciation

Ⓐ Look at Figure 1. Are these sentences true or false? Correct the false sentences.

1	Mars is next to the Sun.	F	Mercury is next to the Sun.
2	Mercury is next to Venus.		
3	Venus is between Mercury and the Earth.		
4	Mars is smaller than Mercury.		
5	Venus is nearer to the Sun than the Earth is.		
6	The Earth is larger than Venus.		
7	The Earth is the largest planet in this group.		
8	Venus is the smallest planet in this group.		

Ⓑ Work in pairs.

1 Find pairs of adjectives in the box opposite.
Example: *far – near*

2 Match each pair of adjectives to a row of information in Table 1 below.
Example: *distance = far / near*

3 Ask and answer questions with *how*. Use adjectives from the box.
Example: *How far is Venus from the Sun?*
It's 108.2 million kilometres.

4 Ask and answer more questions about the planets.
Example: *Which planet is nearest to the Sun?*
It's Mercury.

Table 1: *Comparison of the inner planets*

	Mercury	Venus	The Earth	Mars
Distance from the Sun (m km)	57.9	108.2	149.6	227.9
Diameter (km)	4,878	12,103	12,756	6,786
One 'year' (in Earth days)	88	225	365	687
One 'day' (in Earth days)	58	243	1	1
Weight (Earth = 100%)	5.5%	80%	100%	11%
Min. temp. (°C)	-180	465	-70	-120
Max. temp. (°C)	430	465	55	25

Figure 1: *The inner planets*

cold	far	heavy	hot	large
light	long	near	short	small

C Learn prepositions of place and movement.
Work in groups.

Group 1

Study Figure 2.
Where are all the letters? You can often make several sentences.

Example:

A is next to F. A is near F.

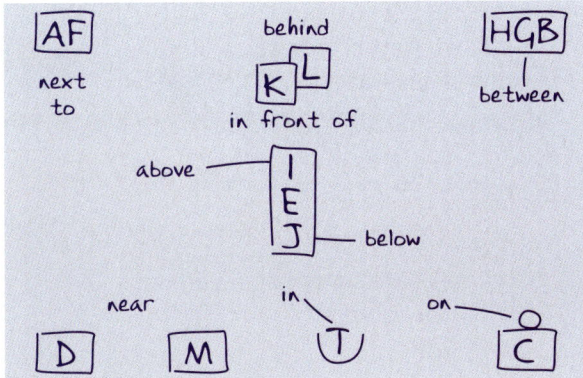

Figure 2: *Prepositions of place*

Group 2

Study Figure 3.
Where are all the numbers going? You can sometimes make two sentences.

Example:

1 is going towards 2.; 2 is going away from 1.

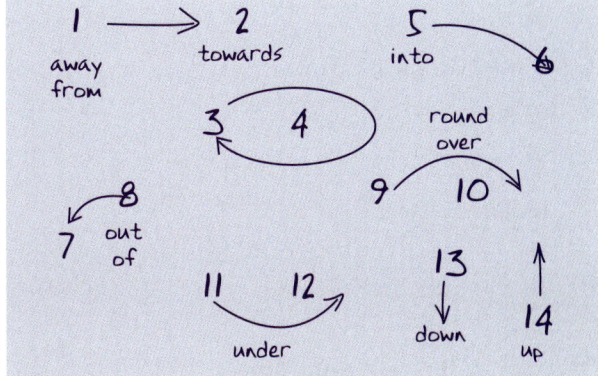

Figure 3: *Prepositions of movement*

D Work in pairs.

Make pairs with a student from the other group in Exercise C. Cover the diagrams above.
Teach your partner about your prepositions.
Use drawings.

E Study the conversation below.

1 Complete the conversation with a preposition in each space.

2 🔘 **2:19** Listen and check your answers.

3 Practise the conversation in pairs.

4 Ask for directions to other places.

Pronunciation Check 2

Saying prepositions of place and movement

Make sure you say the words and phrases with the correct stress.

First syllable	Second syllable
'under	a'bove
'over	be'hind
'into	be'low
'out of	be'tween
'next to	a'way from
	to'wards

🔘 **2:18** Listen and repeat each sentence.

A: Where's the nearest bank?
B: It's _____ the park. Go _____ the hill.
A: _____ the city centre?
B: No, _____ from the centre. Go _____ the bridge and _____ the corner. It's _____ the post office and the supermarket.
B: Is there a car park?
A: Yes. The car park is _____ the bank.
B: Can you park _____ the street?
A: Sometimes. There are some spaces _____ the supermarket.

Lesson 4: Reading

A Complete each word to make a list of geographic features.

1 se a_____
2 mou_____
3 ri_____
4 la_____
5 oc_____
6 is_____
7 be_____
8 de_____
9 fo_____
10 ju_____

B Do the quiz on the right.

C Look at the text opposite.

1 Read the heading and the introduction. Which topics in the quiz are in the text?

2 Scan each paragraph. Find the names of two places in each paragraph.
Example: *Australia*

D Work in groups.

1 Read about one of the topics in the text. Find the answer to one or two questions in the quiz. Find extra information about the answer(s).

2 Give your information to the other people in your group.

E Look at the highlighted sentences in the text.

Find and underline the introductory phrases. Circle the subject of the sentence. Box the verb.

F Talk about the text.

What is the most interesting or surprising piece of information?

GEOGRAPHY QUIZ
How good is your geography?
Do our quiz and find out.

What is:
- the longest river?
- the deepest lake?
- the largest ocean?
- the largest desert?
- the biggest continent?
- the smallest continent?
- the largest rainforest?

Skills Check 1

Dealing with long sentences (2)

Sentences sometimes begin with an introductory phrase.

Examples:
Some websites say that …
the longest river in the world is the Nile.
All reference books agree that …
the Amazon is the largest river.

Look for the word *that* at the end of the introductory phrase. The subject of the sentence is the next word.

Sometimes, writers do not use *that* at the end of the introductory phrase.

Researchers believe	
The experiment showed	(that)
Aristotle thought	

Learn to recognize introductory phrases. Find the subject and verb of the sentence after the introductory phrase.

Skills Check 2

Superlative adjectives (2)

With long adjectives, we put *the most* in front of the adjective.

Examples:

interesting	the most interesting
surprising	the most surprising

OBJECTIVES
- deal with long sentences: introductory phrases
- recognize superlative adjectives with *most*
- read a text about extremes

The biggest, the longest, the deepest

How much do you know about the Earth? Which is the biggest continent, the longest river, the deepest lake and the largest ocean? Read on ... the answer is not always clear.

Continents

The largest continent in the world is Asia. It is 44.8 million square kilometres. Some people believe that the smallest continent is Australia at 7.7 million square kilometres. However, many reference books and websites say that Australia is not a continent. It is part of the continent of Oceania. These sources say that Oceania, including Australia, is the smallest continent. It contains thousands of islands, but the total area is only 8 million square kilometres.

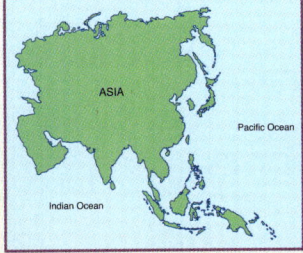

Rivers

Some websites say that the longest river in the world is the Nile, with a length of around 6,650 kilometres. These websites say that the Amazon is shorter, at 6,400. Other people measure the Amazon at 6,992 kilometres and the Nile at 6,853. However, all reference books and websites agree that the *largest* river is the Amazon. It sends 219,000 cubic metres of water into the Atlantic Ocean every second. The Nile is much smaller, at 5,100 cubic metres per second. The Amazon is also the widest river in the world.

Lakes

The largest lake in the world is not called a lake. It is the Caspian Sea in Asia and Europe. It has an area of 371,000 square kilometres. The deepest lake is Lake Baikal in Siberia. It has an average depth of 630 metres, but its deepest point is 1,637 metres. Scientists say that Lake Baikal contains 20% of the world's unfrozen fresh water.

Oceans

The Pacific Ocean is the biggest ocean in the world. It covers almost a third of the Earth's surface. It stretches from the Arctic in the north to Antarctica in the south. It is divided into the North Pacific and the South Pacific. Researchers say that the deepest part of the Pacific is south of Japan. It is the Mariana Trench with a depth of 10,924 metres. The smallest ocean is the Arctic Ocean. At 13,223,800 square kilometres, it is ten times smaller than the Pacific.

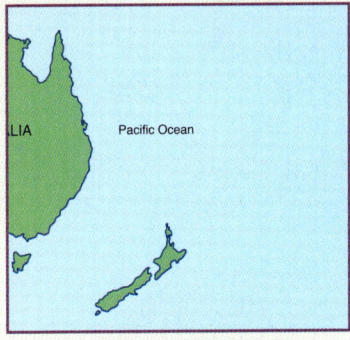

Lesson 5: Writing and Grammar

Ⓐ Study the letters in the first column below. Then add letters to make an adjective and a noun.

		adjective	noun
1	w__d__	wide	width
2	l__ng		
3	d___p		
4	str__ng		
5	h__gh		

Ⓑ Look at Table 1 and Table 2.

1 Find the patterns. Complete the tables.

2 Draw and write another example in the final row of each table.

Ⓒ Write a sentence for each drawing below. Use patterns from the Skills Check.

44.8 m km²

Asia

1 Asia covers 44.8 million square kilometres.

The Nile

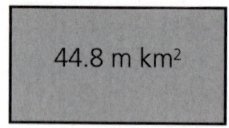

6,825 km

2

The Amazon

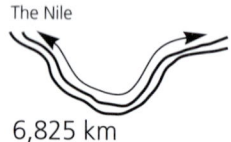

11 km at the coast

3

Lake Baikal

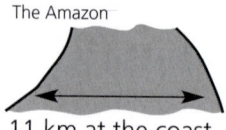

1,637 m

4

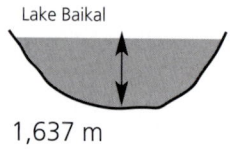

Table 1: *Area*

Drawing	L	H	___	Words
6 m / 4 m	6 m	4 m	24 m²	twenty-four square metres
10 km / 5 km	10 km	__ km	50 km²	_____ square kilometres
20 cm / 3 cm	__ km	3 cm	60 cm²	sixty _____ centimetres

Table 2: *Volume*

Drawing	L	H	W		Words
6 m / 4 m / 2 m	6 m	2 m	4 m	48 m³	forty-eight cubic metres
10 km / 5 km / 3 km	10 km	__ km	5 km	150 km³	_____ cubic kilometres
20 cm / 2 cm / 3 cm	_____	3 cm	2 cm	120 cm³	one hundred and twenty ___ centimetres

Table 1: Superlative adjectives (1)

| The Amazon | _____ | _____ | widest | river | in the world. |
| The Rockies | _____ | _____ | highest | | in North America. |

Table 2: Superlative adjectives (2)

| Hydrogen | _____ | _____ | _____ | common | gas | in the Solar System. |
| Red diamonds | _____ | _____ | _____ | expensive | jewels | on Earth. |

D **Look at the tables.**

1 What do we use superlative adjectives for? Tick (✓) one use.

- to talk about one thing ▢
- to compare two things ▢
- to compare many things ▢

2 Complete the tables.

3 Make the superlative sentences into *yes/no* questions.
Example: *Is the Amazon the widest river in the world?*

4 Make the superlative sentences into *wh~* questions.
Example: *What is the widest river in the world?*

5 Complete these sentences with something true for your country.
- a. … is the longest river in my country.
- b. … is the largest lake in my country.
- c. … is the highest mountain in my country.
- d. … is the oldest town or city in my country.
- e. … is the biggest city in my country.
- f. … is the wettest month in my country.
- g. … is the hottest month in my country.

6 Work with a partner. Talk about your sentences in question 5.
Do you come from the same country? Have you got the same answers?

7 Complete these sentences with your own opinion. Begin with *I think that …*
- a. … is the most interesting book in my language.
- b. … is the most important person in my country.
- c. … is the most useful website on the Internet.
- d. … is the most beautiful place in my country.
- e. … is the most difficult subject at school/university.
- f. … is the most dangerous animal in the world.
- g. … is the most exciting sport in the world.

8 Tell your partner your opinions from question 7. Begin with *I think that …*

Lesson 6: Writing and Grammar

A Make the words into sentences about geographic features in different countries and continents.

1 Yangtze / long / river / China

The Yangtze is the longest river in China.

2 The Mariana Trench / deep part / Pacific Ocean

_____

_____

3 The Dead Sea / Jordan / low point / Earth

_____

_____

4 Victoria / big / lake / Africa

_____

_____

5 Oceania / small / continent / on Earth

_____

_____

The Yangtze River, China

Mount Kivu, Rwanda

B Study the two sentences below.

Kivu is the highest lake in Africa.

The highest lake in Africa is Kivu.

1 What is the subject of each sentence?

2 What is the verb?

3 What is the complement?

4 Do the two sentences give the same information?

C Rewrite the sentences in Exercise A above. Reverse the order of the subject and the complement.

1 The longest river in China is the Yangtze.

2 _____

_____

3 _____

_____

4 _____

_____

5 _____

_____

Skills Check

Reversing subject and complement

We can reverse the **subject** and the **complement** in sentences with a **definite** complement. The two sentences have the same meaning.

Example:

S	V	C
The Sahara	is	**the** largest desert in the world.
The largest desert in the world		the Sahara.

Note: We cannot reverse with an indefinite complement, e.g., *Russia is **a** country.*

OBJECTIVES
• reverse the subject and complement
• write a description of a geographic feature

D Read the sentences and the questions. (Circle) the correct word or phrase in each case.

1	The nearest planet to the Sun	it is (is)	Mercury.
2	Lake Baikal is	640 kilometres long. a length of 640 kilometres.	
3	It is	deepest lake the deepest lake	in the world.
4	The Himalayas appeared	before 25 million years. 25 million years ago.	
5	How long When	ago	did the Himalayas appear?
6	Some websites	tell that say that	Australia is a continent.
7	How	short tall	are you?
8	The Earth is	between next	Mars and Venus.
9	The train went	below under	the bridge.
10	The supermarket is	near to next to	the bank.

E Read the encyclopedia text about islands. Complete the island column.

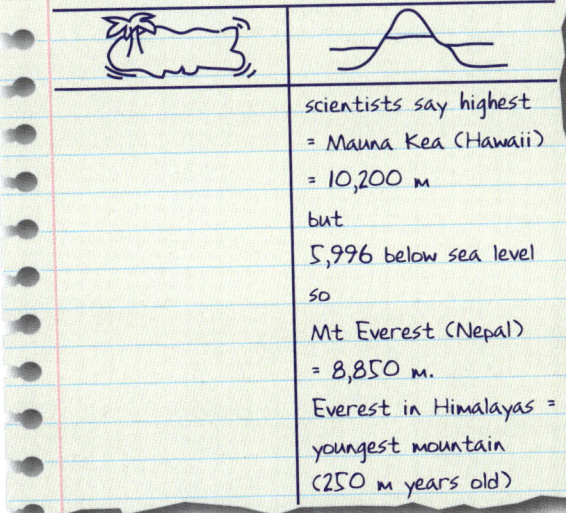

scientists say highest
= Mauna Kea (Hawaii)
= 10,200 m
but
5,996 below sea level
so
Mt Everest (Nepal)
= 8,850 m.
Everest in Himalayas =
youngest mountain
(250 m years old)

ISLANDS

Some encyclopaedias say that the largest island in the world is Australia. It is in the southern hemisphere. It covers 7.7 million square kilometres.

However, some websites say that Australia is not called an island, because it is a continent. These websites say that Greenland is the largest island. It has an area of 2.2 million square kilometres.

The youngest island in the world* is Surtsey near Iceland in the North Atlantic ocean. It covers 3.2 square kilometres. It appeared above the sea 40 years ago.

* as of January 2010

Figure 1: *Mount Everest and Mauna Kea*

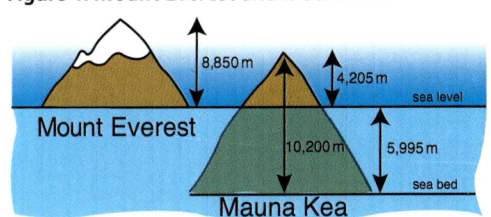

F Look at Figure 1 and read the notes about mountains. Write an encyclopedia text. Use some patterns from this unit.

At the end of Unit 5, I can:

☐ recognize key words in a lecture

☐ talk about factual information in the past

☐ apply pronunciation rules in the unit

☐ use introductory phrases to aid comprehension of long sentences

☐ describe dimensions in writing

☐ use the grammar of the unit accurately

Transfer

Think about how you could use what you have learnt in this unit to talk about your own country.

Reflect

Think about the things you have seen, heard or read in your life. What are the best, biggest, funniest, most interesting things? Add an appropriate superlative to the things you have thought of.

Review

Lesson 1: Listening

1 a dr_____

ITALY

Adriatic Sea

Croton

Tyrrhenian Sea

Ionian Sea

Mediterranean Sea

2 a ma_____

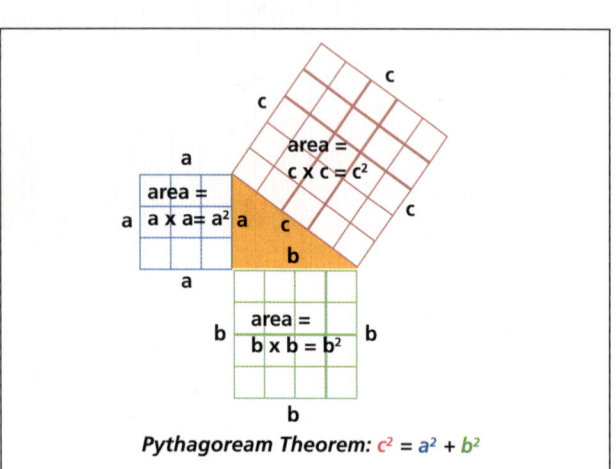

c

c

area =
c X c = c²

area =
a x a= a² a c c

b

a

area =
b x b = b² b

b

b

Pythagoream Theorem: $c^2 = a^2 + b^2$

3 a di_____

4 a ph_____

Ⓐ Look at the items above.

1 Complete the names of the items.

2 What can you see in the items above? Tick (✓) some of the words and phrases.

a brown circle		a formula		a ladder	
a nose		a purple line		a triangle	
a yellow triangle		blue squares		fur	
green squares		hair		red triangles	
skin		smoke		a building	
some cities		some countries		some islands	
some mountains		the Sun			

3 What is the connection between the four items? Guess!

B 🔘 **2:20 Listen to the introduction to a lecture about the man in the drawing. Number the topics in order. (There are some extra topics).**

Life in Ancient Greece	
Life in Ancient Rome	
The life of Pythagoras	
Real life uses of Pythagoras' Theorem	
The famous formula of Pythagoras	
Other famous formulas	
The lives of other famous Greek mathematicians	

C 🔘 **2:21 Listen to the first part of the lecture. Number the next piece of information in each case.**

Example: *1 His hometown was Samos in Greece, but …*

he had to leave Croton in about 508 BCE.	
he did not live his whole life in his birthplace.	*1*
he didn't like the king of the region. He went to a place called Croton in Italy.	
he wanted to teach people his ideas.	
he thought that Mathematics was the most important subject.	
many people came to learn at his school.	

D 🔘 **2:22 Listen to the second part of the lecture.**

1 Follow the lecturer's instruction.

2 What is the answer to the question at the end?

E 🔘 **2:23 Listen to the third part of the lecture.**

1 Make a diagram of the example.

2 Work out the length of the ladder.`

F 🔘 **2:24 Listen to the stressed syllables of some words from the lecture. Number the word in each case.**

formula		region		famous	
important		triangle		area	
building		answer		science	
subject		interesting		describe	

A **Describe the pictures. Use the nouns, adjectives and verbs below. Make any necessary changes.**

boy	bus	bus stop	canteen	girl	hair
iPod	morning	people	beautiful	black	blue
brown	green	old	pretty	red	yellow
answer	ask	drink	eat	listen	rain
sit	stand	talk			

Example: *In the first picture, there is a boy and a girl. They are about 18 years old …*

B Study the conversations.

1 Complete each conversation with a word in each space.

2 🔘 **2:25** Listen and check your answers.

3 Role-play the conversations in pairs.

4 Add some more lines to each conversation.

A: It's cold _____.

B: Yes, it _____.

A: And it's raining. I hate _____.

B: Actually, I like _____. But I don't like cold _____.

A: It was warmer _____.

B: Yes. Warm and _____.

A: _____ you at the university?

B: Yes, I _____. I'_____ in the first year. What about you?

A: I'm in the first year, too.

A: What are you _____?

B: English Literature.

A: _____ are you doing that?

B: I want to _____ an English teacher. And you?

A: I'm _____ to be an engineer.

A: Hi. _____ are you?

B: Fine, _____.

A: Do you always have lunch in the _____?

B: No, I sometimes bring _____ from home.

A: Where do you _____?

B: _____ North Street. _____ to the supermarket. What about you?

A: I _____ near London Road. There are some flats _____ the bank.

A: _____ time do you finish today?

B: The lecture ends _____ 3.45.

A: Are you going to _____ the bus to town?

B: Yes. There's one at _____ 4.00.

A: _____'s at 4.05, actually. I sometimes get that _____.

C Work in pairs.

1 Write one more conversation between the boy and the girl.

2 Practise your conversation.

3 Role-play your conversation for the other students.

Lesson 3: Vocabulary and Pronunciation

A **Look at the photographs. Each one represents a study subject.**

1 What can you see in each photograph?

Example: *1 rainbow, mountains …*

2 Name the subjects.

Example: *History*

3 Think of three words connected with each subject.

Example: *History – kings, queens, dates*

4 Think of three facts from each subject.

Example: *The Second World War ended in 1945.*

B **Look at the words in the left column below.**

1 Find a word in the right column with the same (underlined) vowel sound.

2 🔘 **2:26** Listen and check your answers.

1	a<u>u</u>tumn		deep
2	b<u>ear</u>	I	draw
3	br<u>u</u>sh		hair
4	b<u>ui</u>lder		high
5	cl<u>i</u>mate		s<u>ea</u>son
6	cl<u>ou</u>dy		sh<u>o</u>wer
7	<u>ea</u>st		skill
8	expl<u>ai</u>n		s<u>u</u>nny
9	l<u>ei</u>sure		wake
10	r<u>eg</u>ion		west

C Look at the words in the left column below.

1 Tick (✓) the column with the correct stress pattern.

2 🔊 **2:27** Listen and check.

3 Say the words with the correct pronunciation.

		O o	o O	O o o	O o o o	o O o o	o o O o
1	prepare		✓				
2	triangle						
3	compulsory						
4	application						
5	yesterday						
6	communicate						
7	reference						
8	interesting						
9	trainee						
10	independent						
11	advertisement						
12	tropical						
13	temperature						
14	between						
15	agriculture						

D Match each verb with a noun phrase.

1	evaluate	a bus
2	make	a flow chart
3	draw	a presentation
4	prepare	angry
5	have	breakfast
6	keep	in touch
7	clean	information
8	get	notes
9	do	research
10	catch	your teeth

E Write the opposite of each word or phrase.

1 get up   *go to bed*

2 wake up   _____

3 before   _____

4 employer   _____

5 punctual   _____

6 always   _____

7 qualified   _____

8 thick   _____

9 above   _____

10 into   _____

Lesson 4: Reading

A **Look at the start of each word. What is the complete word?**

1	seasons	su_mmer_	aut___	wi____	sp____
2	continents	Af____	As__	Eu____	No___ Am_____
3	planets	Ma___	Ve___	Ju_____	Sa____
4	animals	co_	be__	do_	gi_____
5	jobs	cl___	fa____	ma_____	nu___
6	employment sectors	ag_____	ma_____	re____	fi_____

B **Choose a word from the box to complete each sentence below.**

> university survival metres research jobs deep language ~~million~~ environment websites

1 The population of Sao Paolo in Brazil is more than 20 _million_____.

2 All students in Australian secondary schools study a foreign _____.

3 Before the Internet, people used their own books to do _____.

4 Nowadays, sites like Google search hundreds of thousands of _____.

5 People with no qualifications do not usually get good _____.

6 Well-qualified people usually start a career after _____.

7 Animals adapt to survive in an _____.

8 Adaptation is the key to _____.

9 Lake Baikal is 1,637 metres _____.

10 The Nile has a length of around 6,700 _____.

C **You are going to read the text on the opposite page. It is from a website for students.**

1 Look at the heading, the photographs and the maps. What is the text about?

2 Read the introduction. What topics are in the text? In what order?

3 Work in groups.

  a Read one of the sections each, e.g., Student 1 reads *The hottest*. Make notes of the important information in your section.

  b Ask each other questions to find out more information.

  Example: *Where is the windiest place on Earth?*

  Use your notes to answer questions. Guess the pronunciation of the names in your section.

4 Where are these places? Find the information quickly by looking at the whole text.

  a. Al'Azziziya   d. The Atacame Desert

  b. Dallol   e. Cherrapunji

  c. Vostok   f. Mount Washington

Big, bigger, the biggest

In this article, we look at world records for temperature, rainfall and wind.

The hottest

On average, the hottest place in the world is the city of Dallol in Ethiopia, a country in East Africa. This city has an average temperature of 34.6°C. However, this temperature is not the highest ever recorded. The town of Al'Aziziyah in Libya is in the edge of the Sahara Desert and the temperature in the town reached 58°C on 13th September 1922.

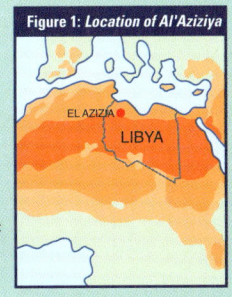

Figure 1: *Location of Al'Aziziya*

The coldest

On average, the coldest place in the world is Plateau in Antarctica. It is not a town, but a research station. It has an average temperature of -56.7°C. However, this temperature is not the lowest ever recorded. The Research Station at Vostok is near the South Pole and the temperature at the station reached -89.2°C on 21st July 1983.

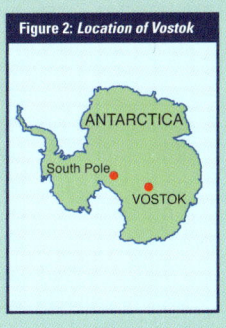

Figure 2: *Location of Vostok*

The wettest

On average, the wettest place in the world is the village of Cherrapunji in India. It has an average rainfall of 12,649 mm a year. However, this rainfall is not the highest ever recorded. Mount Waialeale is in Hawaii in the Pacific Ocean and the region recorded 1,870 mm in a 24-hour period from March 15th to 16th, 1952.

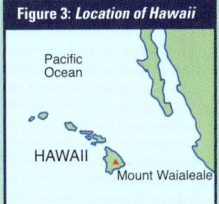

Figure 3: *Location of Hawaii*

The driest

Some websites say that the Atacama Desert in South America is the driest place on Earth. On average, the region has 1 mm of rain per year. However, the driest place in the world is Antarctica. There has been no rain on this continent for at least two million years. Water in the air freezes and becomes ice so it never rains.

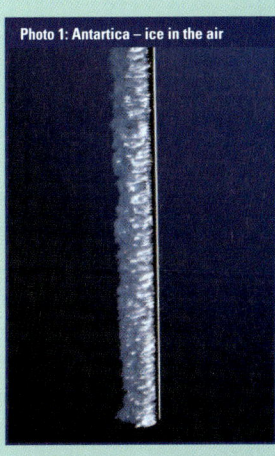

Photo 1: Antartica – ice in the air

The windiest

Some websites say that Mount Washington in the United States is the windiest place on Earth. The record wind speed is 370 kph. However, on average, the windiest place in the world is Antarctica. The continent often has winds of 300 kph. These winds start on the mountains of Antarctica. Cold air flows down these mountains and gets faster and faster.

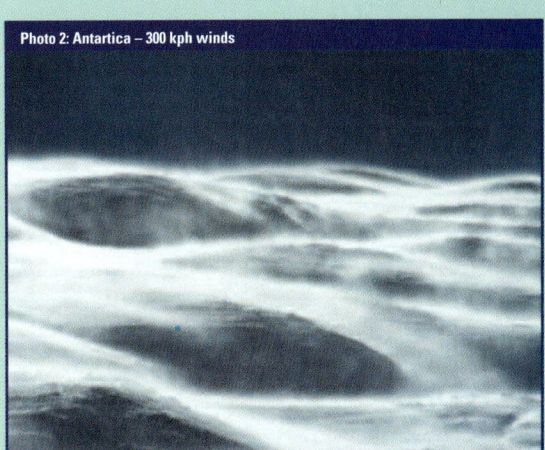

Photo 2: Antartica – 300 kph winds

Lesson 5: Writing and Grammar

A Complete each word with the correct vowels.

1 d a n g e r o u s
2 r___t_n__
3 d___gr__m

4 g___gr__phy
5 h_m_d
6 s___th

7 __s___lly
8 y___ng
9 b_____t_f_l

10 d__ff__c__lt
11 __xp_r__m__nt
12 m_n___l

B Complete each word with doubled letters.

1 a _s_ _s_ ignment
2 a____licant
3 co____unicate

4 employ____
5 ho___y
6 profe___ional

7 va____ey
8 m___n
9 a____istant

10 o____ice
11 bo____om
12 betw____n

C Complete each word with one or two silent letters.

1 autu_m_n
2 assi__nment
3 b__ilder

4 fact__ry
5 lit__rature
6 reg__on

7 comf____table
8 wei____t
9 advertis__ment

10 __sychology
11 s__ience
12 __nowledge

D Look at Figure 1.

1 Where does the graph come from?

2 What does it show?

3 How much do doctors earn each year, on average? What about factory workers?

4 What is the missing information? Guess!

E Look at the text about the graph.

1 Complete the text with a preposition in each space.

2 Complete the graph with information from the text.

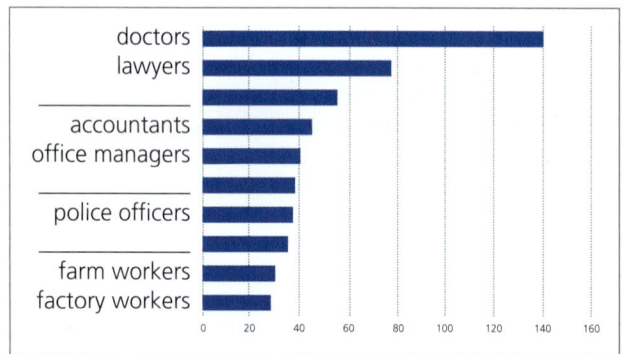

Figure 1: *Average annual salaries in the USA, 2010 (in US $ 000)*
Source: http://www.payscale.com/research/US/

A recent survey _in___ the United States looked _____ average salaries _____ ten jobs. Doctors get the highest salary _____ this group. _____ average, they earn US $140,000 per year. Lawyers are _____ second place. They receive about half the salary _____ doctors. Nurses are third, _____ accountants and office managers. Lorry drivers and police officers are on similar salaries of about US $38,000. Shop assistants and farm workers come _____ police officers. Factory workers are _____ the bottom _____ the list. They get around US $28,000 per year.

F **Read the sentences and the questions below.**
Tick (✓) the correct sentences and questions. Correct the wrong ones.

1	Are you working at the moment?	✓
2	When are children learning to read in your country?	When do children learn to read in your country?
3	Last week, we learnt drawing graphs.	
4	We learnt about the Second World War yesterday.	
5	I am never late for work.	
6	Sometimes, we have assignments at the weekend.	
7	She writes to her parents every weeks.	
8	How usually do you go out in the evenings?	
9	I don't would like a job in a bank.	
10	I am going to work for the government.	
11	Where are you going to live next year?	
12	What do you want to do after university?	
13	There is three reasons for the problem.	
14	African elephants are the bigger than Asian elephants.	
15	They are the largest land animals on Earth.	
16	There only are about one and a half million African elephants in the world.	
17	In my country, it rains in spring and it also rains in autumn.	
18	The nearest planet to the Earth is Venus.	
19	Venus is in the between Mercury and the Earth.	
20	When ago did the African continent appear?	

Lesson 6: Portfolio

You are going to do some research, make a poster or a set of PowerPoint slides, and give a short talk in groups.

Ⓐ Understand the task.

1 Look at the photographs on the opposite page. Answer the questions.

    a. What does each ring on a tree represent?

    b. What information can you get from an ice core?

    c. What does a thermometer measure?

    d. What does smoke from a factory contain?

2 Look at the graph on the opposite page. Match the questions and answers.

1	What is the horizontal scale?		this year
2	What is the left-hand vertical scale?		about 18,000 years ago
3	What is the right-hand vertical scale?	*I*	years ago
4	What does the red line show?		tree rings, ice cores and thermometers
5	What does the blue line show?		degrees Celsius
6	What does 0 at the bottom right mean?		average temperature
7	When did CO_2 reach the highest point?		about 300,000 years ago
8	When did average world temperature reach the lowest point?		CO_2 parts per million
9	Where does the information in the graph come from?		CO_2 in the atmosphere

3 What is the most interesting information in the graph?

Ⓑ Do research and communicate information

What is the explanation for the rise in average world temperature? You are going to read about a possible reason.

1 Work in groups of four. Make notes on a text.

    Student 1: Read about **the Sun**.   **Student 3**: Read about **cars**.

    Student 2: Read about **cows**.   **Student 4**: Read about **trees**.

2 Give your information to your group.

3 Which reason do you think is correct?

Ⓒ Prepare a poster.

What can we do about the rise in average world temperature?

1 Think of one or two solutions.

2 Put the main points on a poster or some PowerPoint slides.

D **Give a talk.**

1 Practise talking about your solutions.

2 Give your talk to the other students.

tree rings

an ice core

a thermometer

smoke from factories

Figure 1: *Average world temperature and CO₂ in the atmosphere*

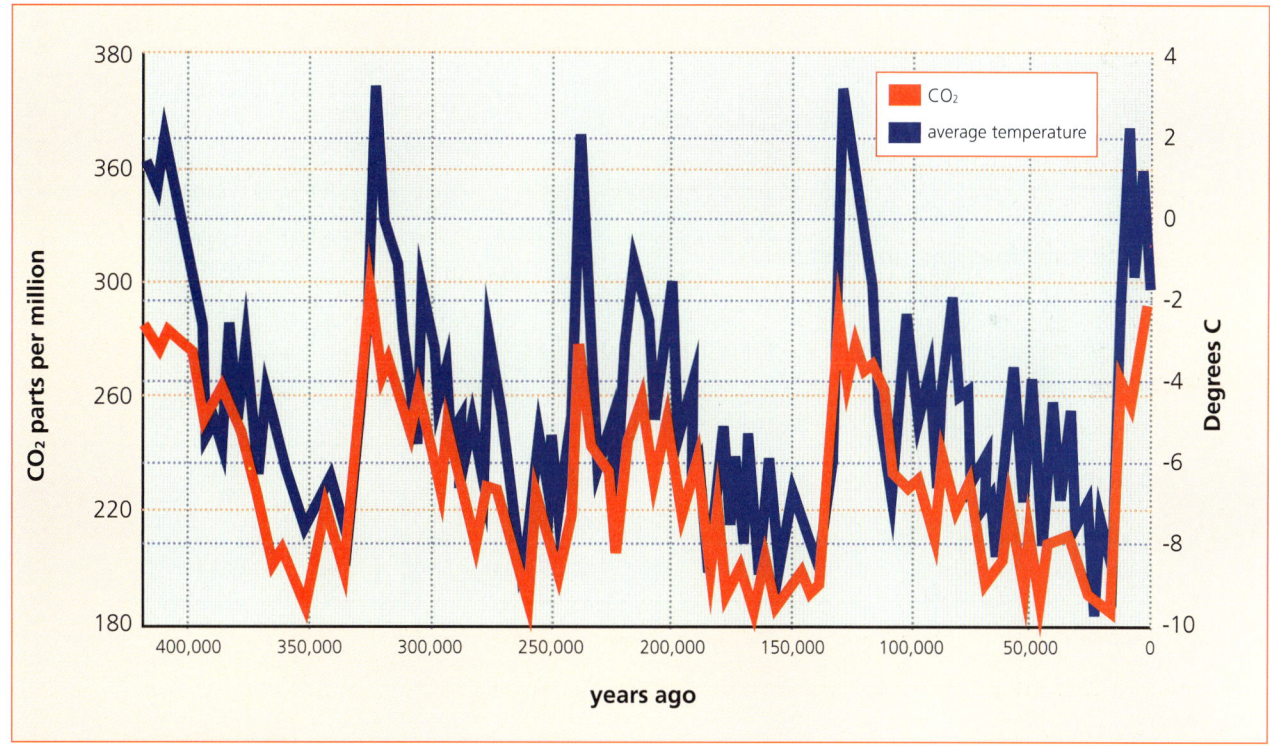

Listening and Speaking

A **Say the words in each box below.**

1 Write the words in the correct column of the correct table on the right.

2 Add one more word to each column.

short vowels

a̲dult	black	bread	does	drink
fish	friend	give	hot	lei̲sure
man	month	sun	want	watch

long vowels

ask	blue	can't	court	first	her
juice	last	mall	move	peo̲ple
read	walk	week	work	

dipthongs

brown	child	cloud	day	go	grey
how	right	road	sky	snow	type

Table 1: *Short vowels*

/æ/	/e/	/ɪ/	/ɒ/	/ʌ/
bank	ten	six	wrong	one

Table 2: *Long vowels*

/ɑː/	/ɜː/	/ɪ/	/ɔː/	/uː/
grass	third	three	four	do

Table 3: *dipthongs*

/ɑɪ/	/eɪ/	/aʊ/	/əʊ/
five	eight	now	no

B **Look at the questions and answers below.**

1 Cover the answers. Think of a suitable reply to each question.

2 Uncover the answers. Write the correct question number next to each answer.

3 🔘 **1:1** Listen and check.

4 Practise the questions and answers in pairs.

1	When do children begin nursery in your country?	⬜		Nowadays, most teenagers go on to university or college.
2	Do all children go to nursery?	⬜		Most children leave at 11. A few children change schools at 12 or 13.
3	When do children leave primary school?	⬜		No. Some children leave then, but most children stay at school for another two years.
4	Where do they go?	⬜		To a secondary school, from 11 to 18.
5	Do all children study the same subjects?	⬜		Yes, they do. For the first three years of secondary school. Then they can choose.
6	When can children leave school?	⬜		No. Most children start school at five.
7	Do most children leave school then?	⬜		When they are 16.
8	What about university or college?	**1**		They begin at three or four.

C Write the *~ing* form of these verbs.

1 learn   *learning*

2 do   _____

3 study   _____

4 sit   _____

5 smile   _____

6 prepare   _____

7 send   _____

8 look   _____

9 explain   _____

10 write   _____

11 go   _____

12 make   _____

D Read the text in the speech bubbles.

1 Write the verbs in brackets in the present continuous tense.

A
I'm an IT student. I___ really _____ (enjoy) my course. At the moment, we___ _____ (study) website design. I___ _____ (write) an assignment about it. My tutor is really nice. She___ _____ (help) me a lot with my assignment at the moment.

B
I___ _____ (study) sociology. There are six students in my tutor group. Two students ___ _____ (study) education and sociology. Two students ___ _____ (prepare) a presentation with me at the moment. They ___ _____ (help) me a lot. They _____ (have) really good ideas.

C
I___ _____ (take) tourism. I___ _____ (not do) much work at the moment. I___ _____ (not feel) well. My friends ___ _____ (take) notes for me this week because I can't go to lectures.

2 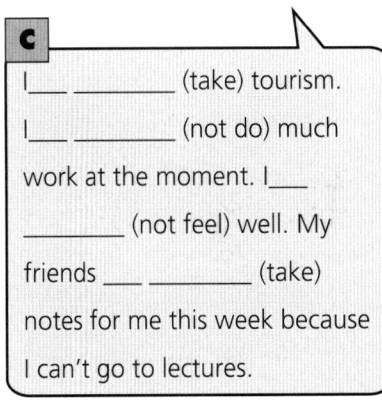 **1:2** Listen and check your answers.

E Circle the correct form of each verb, present simple or present continuous.

1 A: Excuse me. *I look / I'm looking* for my tutor – John Evans.

B: Oh, he's not here today. He*'s working / works* from home.

2 A: Hi! What *are you doing / do you do*?

B: I *send / 'm sending* a text. But there's no signal here.

3 A: Can I use that computer now? *Are you working / do you work* on it?

B: Sorry, give me two minutes. I *just finish / 'm just finishing* something.

4 A: Where's Jane? I want to speak to her.

B: She*'s having / has* a shower, I think.

5 A: Where *do you come / are you coming* from?

B: I'm from Frankfurt, in Germany.

6 A: *Are you speaking / Do you speak* English?

B: Yes, a little.

Reading and Writing

Ⓐ Lucy is 21. She's doing a teacher training course. At the moment, she is studying a Year 3 class. Here is her report. Find and correct the mistakes. There are 20!

I am watch a Year 3 class at Queen Elizabeth Primary School at the moment. The school is old but the buildings is new. He is a mixed school for boys and girls from 7–11. They are about 300 pupils at the school, and they have about 20 teacher. There are 30 child in my class from seven to eight years old. A teacher is Mrs Jones. She 25.

On the morning, the children have lessons in Maths and English. The children usually works in groups. After lunch, they has PE. Sometimes, there paint pictures. I help the children to reading. There is a class library have lots of childrens books. The children can choose two book every week. Sometimes, the children they become noisy but Mrs Jones never shouts.

At the moment, the children is learning about the sea. I am helping they with a wall display. This morning, the children make pictures of fish for the display.

Ⓑ Study the text opposite.

1 Read the heading and the subheading. Look at the figures. What is the text about?

2 What sort of information will you find in the text? Tick (✓) one or more.

- facts from the past ☐
- facts from the present ☐
- predictions for the future ☐
- advice ☐

Ⓒ Read the text opposite. Mark these sentences true (T) or false (F).

1 The name of the symbol π is pi. ☐ T

2 Pi is a Greek letter. ☐

3 π is c/d. ☐

4 You can use pi to find the area of a circle. ☐

5 The value of pi is exactly 3.141519. ☐

6 The Greeks discovered pi. ☐

7 A British man gave pi its name in the 18th century. ☐

8 Pi is not very important today. ☐

It's 3.141519 ... and a bit

What is π? In this article, we look at pi, in the past and today.

All circles have a radius (r), a diameter (d) and a circumference (c) (see Figure 1). The radius is a straight line from the centre to the circumference. The diameter is a straight line from one side to the other. The area of a circle is πr^2. The circumference of a circle is $2\pi r$. But what is π?

Four thousand years ago, the Egyptians discovered π. They looked at circles of different sizes. They looked at the circumference and the diameter. They found something very interesting. The circumference divided by the diameter is always the same number. The number is 3.14. Actually, it is 3.141519… The number never stops. Computers can calculate the number to billions of decimal places, but it goes on forever.

In the 5th century BCE, the Greeks used the number, but they did not give it a name. In 1707, in Britain, William Jones called the number pi. This is a letter from the Greek alphabet. The symbol for the letter is π.

Pi may be the most important number in mathematics. There are thousands of formulas in mathematics with pi. It is the basis of most technology in the world today.

Look at Figure 2. What is the circumference of this circle? What about the area?

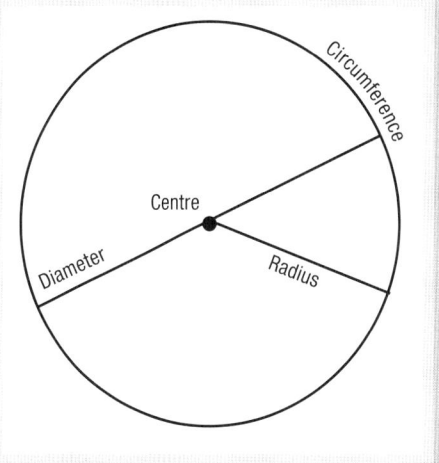

Figure 1: *Important parts of a circle*

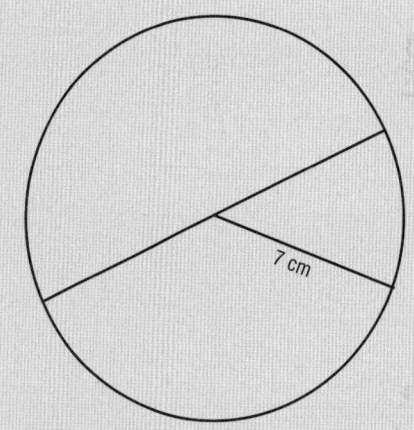

Figure 2: *A circle of radius 7 cm*

D **Answer the questions in one or two sentences each.**

1 What did you learn about in English grammar in this unit?

_____

_____

2 What facts did you learn in this unit?

_____

_____

3 What did you learn to do in this unit?

_____

_____

Listening and Speaking

Ⓐ Study the information in Table 1. It is from a survey about the use of free time.

1 Correct these sentences about Fatima and Mario.

a. Fatima is coming Pakistan.

b. She study English.

c. She likes reading and cook.

d. She watches TV and listens radio.

e. Mario don't use e-mail.

f. He uses the Internet and making voice calls on his cellphone.

g. Fatima and Mario both watches TV.

h. They doesn't send e-mails.

2 Complete the sentences about Hirohito. Use a suitable verb in the correct form.

a. He _____ from Japan.

b. He _____ Economics.

c. He _____ going to the sports centre.

d. He _____ texts and e-mails.

e. He _____ social networking sites.

f. He _____ voice calls.

3 🔘 **1:3** Listen and check. Practise saying the sentences.

4 Make *yes/no* questions about the people in the table. Then listen and check.

a. _____ Hirohito _____ from Japan?   *Does Hirohito come from Japan?*

b. _____ Economics?

c. _____ reading?

d. _____ Fatima _____ – India?

e. _____ cooking?

f. _____ social networking sites?

g. _____ Mario _____ the Internet?

h. _____ texts?

i. _____ football?

5 Ask and answer the questions in 4 in pairs.

Table 1: *How students spend their free time*

	Nationality	Subject	Free time	Digital methods
Fatima	Pakistani	English	reading cooking TV and radio	text voice calls social networking sites
Mario	Italian	Tourism	playing football using the Internet TV	text voice calls
Hirohito	Japanese	Economics	sports centre computer games	e-mail text social networking sites voice calls

B Look at the table below.

1 Choose the correct sentence in each pair.

	A	**B**
1	Where he live?	Where does he live?
2	We go home by bus.	We go to home by bus.
3	I no understand this word.	I don't understand this word.
4	What you do in the evenings?	What do you do in the evenings?
5	I like my lectures very much.	I like very much my lectures.
6	She doesn't go to the lectures.	She don't go to the lectures.
7	I catch the bus at 7.55.	I catch bus at 7.55.
8	I once a week meet my tutor.	I meet my tutor once a week.
9	John sends a lot of texts on him phone.	John sends a lot of texts on his phone.
10	My friend has sandwiches every day.	My friend he has sandwiches everyday.

2 🔘 **1:4** Listen and check.

C Look at the sentences below.

1 Write a verb or auxiliary from the box in each space. You can use the same word more than once. You can use contracted forms, e.g., *I'm*.

> am   'm not   is   are/aren't
>   does/doesn't   do/don't

1. I_____ a teacher. I'm a student.

2. Beijing _____ in China.

3. We _____ going to a lecture today –
   it__ Sunday!

4. What time _____ the lecture start?

5. My father _____ send texts because he
   _____ understand his cellphone.

6. How long _____ teenagers spend on
   computers?

7. They _____ want to do the assignments –
   they _____ too difficult!

8. Where___ the bus? I___ late!

2 🔘 **1:5** Listen and check.

D Look at the sentences below.

1 Make the sentences negative.

1. I spend a lot of time on social networking
   sites.
   *I don't spend a lot of time on social
   networking sites.*

2. My boss sends a lot of e-mails everyday.

3. Teenagers communicate in the same way
   as their parents.

4. Teenagers talk a lot face to face.

5. Beatriz lives in a big house.

6. I watch TV every evening.

7. I always come late.

8. He usually parks his car near the
   supermarket.

9. My mother is always tired in the evenings.

10. You always give me lots of food!

2 🔘 **1:6** Listen and check.

Reading and Writing

A **Match the verbs and the noun phrases.**

1	catch	☐	bed
2	spend	☐	on the phone
3	turn on	☐	Psychology
4	arrive	☐	a lecture
5	go to	☐	an assignment
6	have	☐	a message
7	listen to	☐	home
8	do	☐	a shopping list
9	talk	☐	time
10	send	☐	a meal
11	write	☐	a bus
12	study	☐	the computer

B **Write one of the verbs or verb phrases from Exercise A in each sentence or question.**

1 How long did you _____ on this assignment?

2 How do you _____ this machine?

3 What time do you usually _____ at the university?

4 I don't want to _____ Mathematics any more.

5 What do you usually _____ for dinner?

6 She doesn't usually _____ me e-mails.

7 We always text each other. We don't _____ on the phone.

8 What do you _____ in your free time?

C **Write the words in the correct order to make good sentences or questions.**

1	tired	I	usually	the	am	in	evenings.	
2	always	My	is	for	friend	late	lectures.	
3	to	I	go	sports	never	the	centre.	
4	up	morning.	I	get	on	often	late	Sunday
5	very	She	gives	lectures.	always	interesting		
6	a	dinner.	We	get	takeaway	sometimes	for	
7	like	I	usually	music	don't	rock		
8	usually	Where	you	lunch?	do	have		
9	the	What	does	usually	time	lecture	finish?	
10	you	cinema?	How	do	to	often	go	the

D Study the text below.

1 Read the heading and the subheading. Look at the illustrations. What is the text about?

2 What will the text say about the bad side of the Internet:

a. for research

b. for communication

c. for social life

E Read the text below. Check your predictions from Exercise D2.

The Internet

Is it good or bad? (Part 2)

Last week, we looked at the good side of the Internet. This week, we turn to the bad side. Once again, we consider three areas – research, communication and social life.

Research

Before the Internet, editors always checked the information in a book. Nowadays, a lot of information on the Internet is not checked by anyone. So always check 'facts' on the Internet. Do several websites say the same thing? Then perhaps it is true.

Before the Internet, people used well-known reference books to do research, for example the *Encyclopaedia Britannica*. They also used well-known newspapers like *The New York Times*. Look for well-known names on the website. These websites check their facts.

Before the Internet, you knew something was an advertisement. Nowadays, advertisements on the Internet often pretend to be information. But advertisements often lie. Always get information from *information* websites, not *advertising* websites.

Communication

Before the Internet, people sometimes sent advertisements by post. You always knew that it was an advertisement. Nowadays, people send advertisements in e-mails. You sometimes think it is a real message. Always check the sender's name. If you don't recognize the name, don't open the e-mail. Never click on attachments. Sometimes these *advertisements* can damage your computer.

Social life

Before the Internet, you met people face-to-face. You saw the real age of the person and the sex of the person. On the Internet, people tell you things about themselves. But perhaps they are lying. Never believe people on the Internet. Never tell them any personal information, such as your address. Never arrange to meet anyone face-to-face.

Listening and Speaking

A 💿 **1:7 Listen and complete the flow chart.**

START

Work with hands? → **Yes** → ☐

↓ **No**

Study for a long time? → **Yes** → ☐

↓ **No**

Be in charge? → **Yes** → ☐

↓ **No**

office worker

END

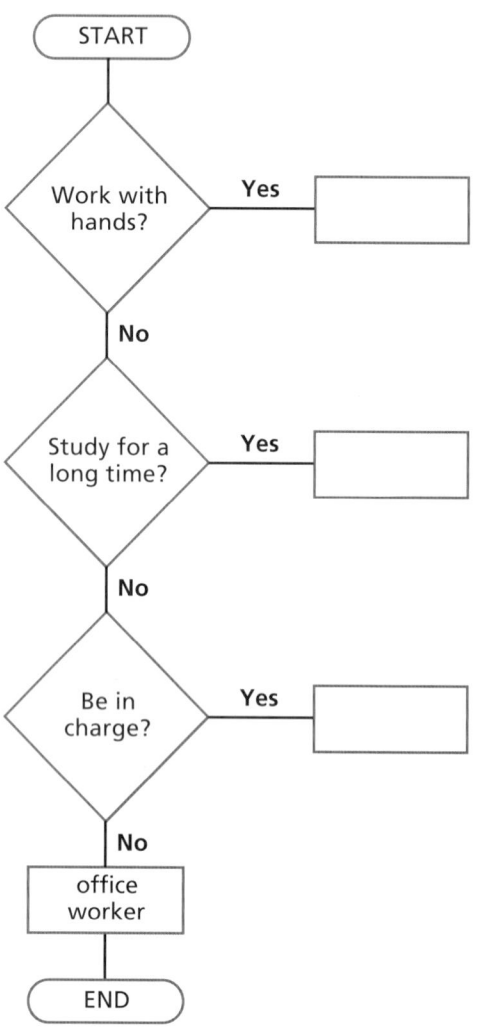

B **Work through the flow chart in pairs.**

Find the correct type of job for your partner.

Example: *manager*

Think of an actual job for your partner.

Example: *manager of a shop*

C Match the adjectives and nouns in column one with a noun in column two.

1	high	advertisement
2	long	certificate
3	manual	clerk
4	interesting	hours
5	secondary	industry
6	career	job
7	leisure	person
8	job	plan
9	organized	salary
10	bank	worker

1:8 Listen and check.

D Complete each sentence with one word in the space.

1 He _____ to work with his hands.

2 She _____ like to be a teacher.

3 They are _____ to go to university.

4 I want _____ interesting job.

5 I _____ want to be in charge.

6 _____ you want to work outside?

7 _____ you like to be a manager?

8 _____ you going to go on to university?

9 _____ is he going to do after university?

10 _____ is she going to live?

1:9 Listen and check.

E **1:10 Listen. Number the best word or phrase to complete the questions.**

to lots of different places?	
computers?	
things?	
hands?	
dangerous?	
of money in your job?	
a factory?	
charge of people?	
outside?	1
a lot of people?	
your job?	
the government?	

Reading and Writing

A **Read the start of the case study below. Then read some more sentences from the case study. Who is each sentence about? Write Ellie (E) or Rose (R).**

Case Study

Ellie left school at 16. She got a job in a supermarket. She put food and drinks on the shelves.

Rose stayed on at school then she went to university. She studied hard every day, in the evenings and at the weekends.

1 She got a good job after university, but the company closed down after one year. ___

2 She didn't have exams anymore. ___

3 She didn't have homework in the evenings or at the weekend. ___

4 She had a degree so she got another job very quickly. ___

5 She had lots of exams. ___

6 She had lots of money for clothes and CDs. ___

7 She lost her first job because the supermarket closed down. ___

8 She never had any money for clothes or CDs. ___

9 She passed all the exams and she got a degree. ___

10 She was often very tired and very stressed. ___

B **Complete each sentence with *because* or *so*.**

1 Ellie is looking for a new job _____ she spends a lot of time on job websites.

2 Rose studied hard _____ she wanted good grades.

3 Ellie didn't stay at school _____ she wanted to earn money.

4 Ellie doesn't have enough money for her own apartment _____ she doesn't earn very much.

5 Rose earns a good salary _____ she has a car.

Alan Armstrong
132, Eastvale Road
Morton
AF3 7GH
01745 234 567

Personal profile
I am 20 years old. _____ I am studying at Hadford University at the moment. I am hard-working. I get jobs in the university holidays to help my family. _____

Education
_____
2000–2009 Kingland Secondary School, Morton

Qualifications
6 GCSEs
3 A levels

Skills / achievements
• full driving licence
• _____
• food safety course (Level 1)

Work experience
Summer 2010   **Waiter**
                     Bell's Restaurant, Morton
                     I was responsible for serving food and drinks to seven tables.
                     I learnt to operate the till and to use a credit card machine.

Christmas 2009   **Kitchen assistant**
                     The Grand Hotel, Morton
                     _____

Summer 2009   **Assistant manager**
                     The Starz Bar
                     I organized the staff timetable. I served food and drink. I operated the till and I completed the end of day accounting form.

Hobbies and interests
I enjoy all types of sport. _____ I also like acting.

⊙ Study the resume above. Then add the extra information from the box below to the correct section.

first aid certificate
I am British.
I am confident. I am a member of the local theatre company.
alanarm@hotmail.com
I like reading.
I prepared food. I checked the levels of food and drink every day.
1993–2000 Eastvale Primary School, Morton

Ⓓ Write your own resume. Use the headings from the resume above.

Listening and Speaking

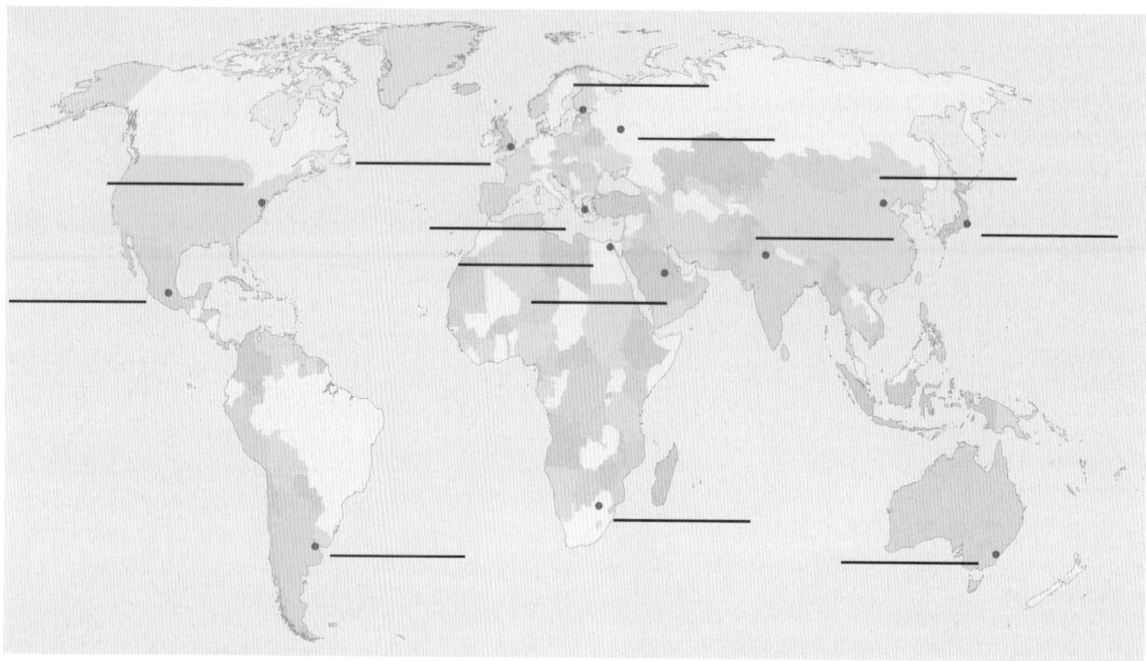

Ⓐ **Study the world map.**

1 Can you guess some of the cities that are marked?

2 Can you guess the country each city is in?

Ⓑ **You are going to hear a talk about weather.**

1 🔘 **1:11** Listen to the first part. Label the map above. Guess the spellings.

2 🔘 **1:12** Listen to the next part. Complete the extract below with *and*, *but*, *because*, *or*.

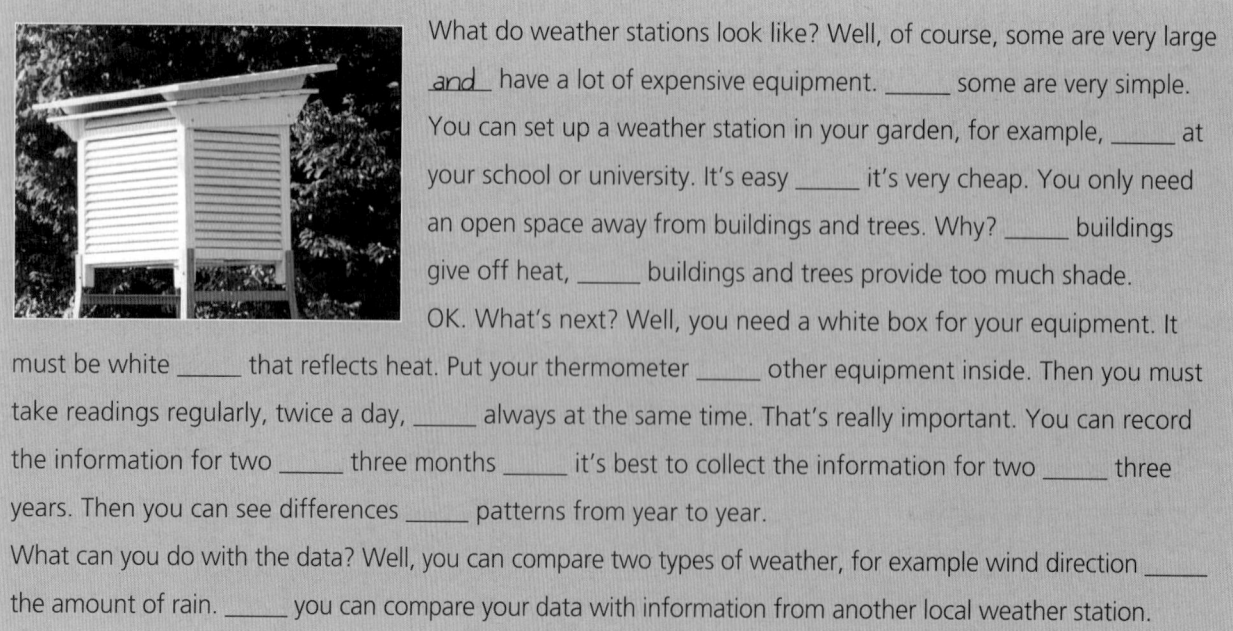

What do weather stations look like? Well, of course, some are very large _and_ have a lot of expensive equipment. _____ some are very simple. You can set up a weather station in your garden, for example, _____ at your school or university. It's easy _____ it's very cheap. You only need an open space away from buildings and trees. Why? _____ buildings give off heat, _____ buildings and trees provide too much shade.

OK. What's next? Well, you need a white box for your equipment. It must be white _____ that reflects heat. Put your thermometer _____ other equipment inside. Then you must take readings regularly, twice a day, _____ always at the same time. That's really important. You can record the information for two _____ three months _____ it's best to collect the information for two _____ three years. Then you can see differences _____ patterns from year to year.

What can you do with the data? Well, you can compare two types of weather, for example wind direction _____ the amount of rain. _____ you can compare your data with information from another local weather station.

C Say the words in the left-hand column.

1 Find words with the same (underlined) vowel sound.

2 🔵 **1:13** Listen and check.

1	trees	August
2	autumn	average
3	cloud	cold
4	snow	flower
5	country	tutor
6	weather	rock
7	humid	climate
8	tropical	summer
9	adapt	terrible
10	ice	season

D Write one word from Exercise C in each sentence. Make any necessary changes. 🔵 **1:14 Listen and check.**

1 It's really cold today. They say it's going to _____.

2 It's really _____ today. Maybe it will rain.

3 In the States, _____ is called 'fall'.

4 In Britain, the weather is often cold, wet and _____.

5 Which _____ are you from?

6 What was the _____ like on your holiday?

7 It was _____. It rained nearly every day.

8 Do they have a dry _____ in the rainforest?

9 Animals can't _____ quickly to the environment.

10 I tripped over a _____.

E Find and correct 16 mistakes in this extract from a tutorial about the Sherpa people.

A: Now, what you can tell us about the Sherpa people?

B: Well, first, some geography. They live near the Himalayan mountains in Nepal. It's the biggest mountain range in the world. Some are coming from Tibet and India.

C: Sorry. What means *range*?

B: It's a group of mountains.

C: OK. Thanks. Go in.

A: What is like the weather?

B: Well, Nepal have two different climates. There's a mountain climate in the mountains, of course. But most of the country has tropical.

A: Interesting.

B: Oh, I forget to say. Nepal has four seasons. In the wet season, they can to have 375 millimetres of rain.

C: Another thing?

B: There are much animals – yaks, deer and wolves. They have also tigers, rhinos, snow leopards, pandas and elephants. But its numbers are very small.

A: How are they adapt to their environment?

B: The Sherpa people live at a very higher altitude in the summer. But in winter, they go down at the lower parts of the country.

🔵 **1:15** Listen and check.

Reading and Writing

Ⓐ Complete each word. All the words are connected with nature. Sometimes there are two words.

1 ada*pt, ptation*   6 des_____   11 min_____   16 sur_____

2 ani_____   7 env_____   12 pla_____   17 tem_____

3 aut_____   8 fore_____   13 sea_____   18 tro_____

4 cam_____   9 hum_____   14 spr_____   19 wea_____

5 cli_____   10 in_____   15 sum_____   20 win_____

Ⓑ Match each feature with an animal.

1	a shell	☐	a brown bear
2	brown fur	☐	a crocodile
3	a long neck	☐	a giraffe
4	green skin	☐	a panda
5	big paws	☐	a polar bear
6	a very long nose	☐	a snake
7	black and white fur	☐	a turtle
8	no legs	☐	an elephant

Ⓒ Read the introduction to an essay.

Number the topics in the correct order.

- the climate of Nepal ☐
- the climate of the Amazon Rainforest ☐
- the geography of Nepal ☐
- the geography of the Amazon Rainforest ☐
- the living things of Nepal ☐
- the living things of the Amazon Rainforest ☐

> *In this essay, I am going to compare two areas of the world. The two places are Nepal and the Amazon Rainforest. I will discuss their geography, climate and living things. First, I will look at Nepal. Then I will talk about the Amazon Rainforest.*

Ⓓ Read the text about Nepal on the opposite page. Make notes in the *Nepal* column of Table 1.

Ⓔ Read the notes about the Amazon Rainforest. Write three paragraphs. Use *only* and *also* in one or more sentences.

Nepal is small country in Asia. It is between India and China. It covers nearly 150,000 square kilometres. The capital of the country is Kathmandu.

Nepal has two climates. In the mountain area, it has a mountain climate. The weather is very cold and it snows for most of the year. The rest of the country has a tropical climate. There are four seasons, including a monsoon season in summer from June to September. The average rainfall is 350 millimetres per year. The average temperature in the capital is 17°C.

The country has many animals. There are large numbers of yaks, wolves and deer in Nepal. There are also tigers, snow leopards, elephants and pandas, but there are only small numbers of these animals.

	Nepal	The Amazon Rainforest
Country or region?	small country	large region
Location		South America – main part in Brazil; also parts in Peru, Venezuela
Size		nearly 7 m sq. km.
Capital		Manaus
Climate		tropical = humid all year
Seasons		2 = long wet, short dry
Av. rainfall p.a.		2,500 mm
Av. temp		26°C (Manaus)
Animals		millions of types! insects: < 200,000 fish: several thousand birds: < 1,000 large animals: < 300 inc. jaguars, crocodiles, monkeys

F Write three sentences. Compare Nepal and the Amazon Rainforest. Use comparative adjectives.

Listening and Speaking

Table 1: *Comparison of the outer planets*

	Jupiter	Saturn	Uranus	Neptune
Distance from the Sun (m km)	778		2,871	4,497
Diameter (km)			51,000	50,000
One year (in Earth years)			84	165
One day (in Earth hours)			17	16
Weight (Earth = 1)			14	17
Temperature (°C)			-210	-210
No. of moons			15	8
Discovered			1781	1846

Figure 1: *The outer planets*

A **You are going to hear a talk about the outer planets.**

1 Look at Figure 1 and Table 1. What are the outer planets? How do you say each name?

2 🔘 **1:16** Listen to the first part of the talk. Write the information in Table 1.

3 Look at Figure 2 and the words in the box below. How is the lecturer going to say each word?

ammonia	core	frozen	hydrogen	ice
liquid	methane	rock	solid	water

4 🔘 **1:17** Listen to the second part. Label Figure 2 with words from the box above.

B **Complete the sentences with one word in each space.**

1 Uranus is 2,871 million kilometres _____ the Sun.

2 Neptune _____ a diameter of 50,000 kilometres.

3 Jupiter _____ round the Sun in twelve Earth years.

4 One day on Uranus is shorter _____ an Earth day.

5 Saturn is _____ heavier than the Earth.

6 The temperature on Neptune is _____ 210 degrees Celsius.

7 Neptune has _____ moons.

8 A man called Herschel discovered Uranus _____ 1781.

🔘 **1:18** Listen and check.

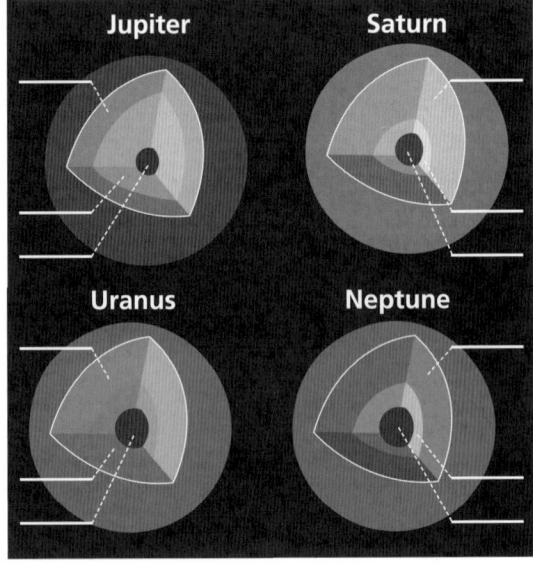

Figure 2: *The cores of the outer planets*

C Complete each sentence with the correct information from Table 1 opposite.

1 The largest planet is _____.

2 The farthest planet from the Sun is _____.

3 Jupiter has the shortest _____ and the shortest _____.

4 Neptune is heavier than _____.

5 The heaviest planet is _____.

6 The lightest planet is _____.

7 Uranus is between _____ and _____.

8 The hottest planet is _____.

9 Saturn is farther from the Sun than _____.

10 The longest day is on _____.

1:19 Listen and check.

D **1:20 Listen. Number the best word or phrase to complete each sentence about the history of the continents.**

Example:
You hear: *1 Today, I'm going to talk to you about the history of the continents.*
Where were the continents million of years ...
You write:

____ continent.

____ continents.

____ moving.

____ ocean.

_1_ ago?

____ parts.

____ places.

____ south.

____ time?

____ today.

____ too.

____ west.

1:21 Listen to the complete sentences and check.

E **Work in pairs or groups. Look again at Table 1.**

1 Describe one planet, but do not give the name. Your partner must work out the name.

2 Compare two planets. Which one is bigger, heavier, etc.

3 Compare all the planets. Which one is the biggest, the heaviest, etc.

fieldtrips4u.com

We organize trips for university students from many different faculties. Just enter your study topic and see the choices. Here is a selection of our most popular field trips this year.

	Sicily	South West USA	Paris
No. of days	5	7	4
Cost	£449	£965	£279
Month	April	May	July
Average temp.	22 °C	17 °C	19 °C
Distance from UK	3.5-hour flight	15-hour flight	2.5-hour train journey
Activities	Visit: • Etna (active volcano) • volcanic islands • Roman ruins	Visit: • Death Valley (desert) • Grand Canyon (river valley) • San Francisco	Visit: • The Pompidou Centre • Notre Dame (cathedral) • Champs Elysee
Study topics	tourism volcanoes mountains rocks coasts human settlements	tourism earthquakes deserts weather coasts water	tourism fine art urban studies city planning public transport culture
Accommodation	Cundari Guest House** Restaurant Swimming pool 30 mins from airport	Holiday Express Hotel*** a/c restaurant pool 75 minutes from airport	Centre Internationale de Paris (Youth centre) Games room TV room 90 mins from airport

Ⓐ Study the website information.

Are these sentences true (T) or false (F)? Correct the false ones.

1	The Paris trip is longer than the Sicily trip.	F	*The Paris trip is shorter than the Sicily trip.*
2	The cheapest trip is the one to Sicily.		
3	Paris is usually hotter in July than Sicily.		
4	It takes longer to get to Sicily than Paris.		
5	All the field trips are useful for Tourism students.		
6	You can visit mountains on the USA trip.		
7	You can swim at the accommodation in Paris.		
8	The accommodation in Sicily is the nearest to the airport.		

B Make a sentence about the three field trips with each adjective in the superlative form.

1 expensive	The USA trip is the most expensive.
2 interesting	
3 exciting	
4 comfortable	
5 dangerous	
6 good for business students	

C Write one word from the box in each space. Make any necessary changes.

ago	between	discuss	~~eclipse~~	forget
heavy	near	pronunciation	solid	under

1 I've never seen an **eclipse** of the Sun.

2 The _____ cash machine is in the High Street.

3 Is an elephant _____ than a rhino?

4 How do you _____ this word?

5 We _____ climate change last week.

6 The Egyptians built the pyramids about 4,000 years _____.

7 The title is usually _____ the figure.

8 Room 240 is _____ the office and the music studio.

9 They can't build there because it is _____ rock.

10 Don't _____ the lecture is at 3.00 today.

D Read the two facts, then write a sentence with a comparative adjective.

1 The Mississippi river is 6,000 km long. The Rhine has a length of 1,320 km.

2 The UK covers 240,000 km^2. Japan has an area of 380,000 km^2.

3 The pyramids at Chichen Itza are about 1,400 years old. The Coliseum in Rome is about 2,000 years old.

4 The average temperature in July in New York is 18°C. In August, it is 19°C.

E Choose the correct sentence in each pair.

	A	B
1	Yesterday was more cold than today.	Yesterday was colder than today.
2	Mercury is smaller that the Earth.	Mercury is smaller than the Earth.
3	Mercury is the most near the Sun.	Mercury is the nearest to the Sun.
4	English is most difficult language.	English is the most difficult language.
5	The Moon is middle of the Sun and the Earth.	The Moon is between the Sun and the Earth.
6	The Earth moves round the Sun.	The Earth moves round from the Sun.
7	He changed his job two years ago.	He changes his job two years ago.
8	How far it is to the university?	How far is it to the university?
9	How heavy is your suitcase?	How light is your suitcase?
10	Which inner planet is the hotter?	Which inner planet is the hottest?

Review

Listening and Speaking

A 🔊 **1:22 Listen and tick (✓) the sentence you hear.**

1 We are doing triangles in Maths at the moment.		We're doing triangles in Maths this week.	
2 We did flow charts in IT yesterday.		We did flow charts in IT last week.	
3 He sometimes plays football in the evenings.		He always plays football in the evenings.	
4 I'm not going to leave school next year.		I'm going to leave school next year.	
5 It is very cold in Antarctica so it doesn't rain.		It is very cold in Antarctica so it snows a lot.	
6 Winter in South America is from June to August.		Winter in North America is from November to February.	
7 Polar bears live in Russia, Greenland and Canada.		Brown bears live in Russia, the USA and Canada.	
8 The deepest lake in the world is Lake Baikal.		The largest lake in the world is the Caspian Sea.	

B **Match the beginning and ending of each question.** 🔊 **1:23 Listen and check your answers.**

1	What do you want to be		at the moment?
2	What are you studying		tomorrow?
3	What do you do		rain?
4	What do you usually have		in your country?
5	What qualifications do you	*I*	after university?
6	What will the weather be like		for lunch?
7	Is it going to		in the summer?
8	What's the average temperature		have?

C **Correct the grammar mistake in each sentence.** 🔊 **1:24 Listen and check your answers.**

1 I reading a good book at the moment. _____

2 Where you are going? _____

3 She gets often angry. _____

4 Do you turn off your phone during lecture? _____

5 Can you to help me with my job application? _____

6 I'd want to work in a hotel. _____

7 What's weather like in your country in the winter? _____

8 Some animals are protecteder than other animals. _____

9 John Couch Adams discovered Neptune 165 years. _____

10 The mantle is between of the outer core and the crust. _____

D **You are going to hear part of a talk about history.**

1 🔘 **1:25** Listen to the introduction. Number the topics in today's talk in order. There are some extra topics.

Africa in the 1800s	
The life of Abraham Lincoln	
Britain in the 1800s	
The problems in the States in the 1860s	
China and Japan in the 1800s	
Europe in the 1800s	
The results of the American Civil War	

2 🔘 **1:26** Listen to the next part of the talk. Choose the best way to complete each sentence.

Example:
You hear: *1 This term in History, we are studying America in the 19ᵗʰ …*
You write:

the United States.	
government.	
died.	
lawyer.	
century.	*1*
year.	
people.	
school.	
1861.	
town.	

E **Discuss in groups.**

How much can you remember about the life of Abraham Lincoln? Make a list of points, then check with the tapescript on page 145.

Reading and Writing

A **Complete each word with the correct spelling.**

1 advant_ _ _ _

2 advertisem_ _ _ _

3 beaut_ _ _ _ _ _

4 comforta_ _ _ _

5 emplo_ _ _ _/_ _ _ _

6 interv_ _ _ _/_ _ _ _ _ _ _

7 prepa_ _ _/_ _ _ _ _ _ _ _

8 sala_ _ _

9 transp_ _ _ _

10 tropi_ _ _ _

11 val_ _ _ _

12 weig_ _

B **Match the words from each column to make phrases.**

1	daily		assistant
2	bank		clerk
3	business		dressed
4	get		networking site
5	go		player
6	keyboard	*1*	routine
7	mp3		school
8	primary		skills
9	social		studies
10	shop		to bed

C **Complete each sentence with words and phrases from the box.**

| Brazil   doctors   teachers   eight million |
| ~~half~~   ~~height~~   Italy   London |
| Portuguese   receptionist   Rome |
| the leisure industry   ~~triangle~~ |

1 The area of a <u>triangle</u> is <u>half</u> base times <u>height</u>.

2 _ _ _ _ _ _ is the capital of _ _ _ _ _ _.

3 The people of _ _ _ _ _ _ speak _ _ _ _ _ _.

4 The population of _ _ _ _ _ _ is about _ _ _ _ _ _.

5 _ _ _ _ _ _ earn more money than _ _ _ _ _ _ in my country.

6 He works in _ _ _ _ _ _. He's a _ _ _ _ _ _.

D **Read *What do computers do?* on the opposite page. Tick (✓) the best way to complete each sentence.**

1 Computers work in this way …

  a. input, process, output ✓

  b. input, output, process ☐

  c. process, input, output ☐

2 To input information, we can use …

  a. a keyboard ☐

  b. a thermometer ☐

  c. a keyboard or a thermometer ☐

3 A *thermometer* tells you …

  a. the time ☐

  b. the temperature ☐

  c. the day ☐

4 Process means …

  a. input ☐

  b. change ☐

  c. information ☐

5 *Output* is …

  a. a noun ☐

  b. a verb ☐

  c. a verb or a noun ☐

6 To output information, we can use …

  a. a monitor or a printer ☐

  b. a monitor ☐

  c. a printer ☐

WHAT DO COMPUTERS DO?

Computers are everywhere nowadays. We use them to study every subject and in our daily lives. They do many different things. But all computer systems have three main stages – input, process, output.

Input is the first stage of any computer operation. We must put information into the computer. There are many ways to input information. For example, we can use a keyboard, and type the information in, or we can connect other things to the computer, like a thermometer. The thermometer can send information about the temperature outside.

Process is the second stage of any computer operation. We must do something with the information. All processes take place in the CPU (central processing unit). The computer changes the information in some way. For example, the CPU can change the information from the keyboard into a computer language. It can put information from a thermometer into a graph of temperature.

Output is the third stage of any computer operation. We must get the information out of the computer. There are many ways to output information. For example, the CPU can put the letters from the keyboard on a monitor. It can send the temperature graph to a printer.

E Read an encyclopedia article about India and complete the *India* column of Table 1.

India

There are three seasons in India. Winter is from November to March. It is warm, but there is snow in the north. Summer is from April to June. It is very hot. The wet season is from June to December on the west coast. It is from October to December on the east coast.

There are four stages of education in India. Fifteen per cent of children go to nursery. All children then go to primary school and secondary school. Ten per cent go on to university or college.

After school or university, 52% of people work in the agriculture sector. Fourteen per cent go into manufacturing or construction. Thirty-four per cent work in finance, retail or the leisure industry. These figures are from 2009.

F Read the notes about China. Write three paragraphs in your notebook in the same format as the text about India.

	India	China
Climate		3 seasons:
win.		Dec-Apr: cool; v. cold in n.
sum.		May-Aug: v. hot
wet		Mar-Apr – s + e June-Aug – w
Education		4 stages:
nurs.		42%
pri.		100%
sec.		100%
uni/coll		23%
Employment		(2008)
agr.		40%
man + con.		27%
fin, ret, lei		33%

Table 1: *Key facts about India and China*

Presenter: 1:1

Unit 1: Education

Lesson 1: Listening

Exercise A. Listen and point.

Voices: Mathematics

History

Geography

IT

Business Studies

Science

diagram

flow chart

bar chart

map

photograph

painting

What time's Business Studies?

Do you have your Science book
with you?

We're doing the 16th century in
History at the moment.

Where's my Geography book?

Do we have Mathematics today?

What did we do in IT last lesson?

I don't understand this diagram.

What does the bar chart show?

Who is this in the painting?

Do you have a better map?

Look at the photograph of a
rainbow.

What does this shape mean, in the
flow chart?

Presenter: 1:2

**Exercise C. Listen and complete
the sentences.**

Teacher 1: Can you get out your IT books?
Page 23. Look at the flow chart.
This is a very simple flow chart. It
is about travelling to [PAUSE]
university.

Teacher 2: OK. Do you have the diagram? In
Maths today, we're going to look
at this diagram. It's very famous.
It's about finding the area of a
[PAUSE] triangle.

Teacher 3: Right. History. Has anyone heard
of Henry VIII? He was king of
England five hundred years ago, in
the 16th [PAUSE] century.

Teacher 4: What are we doing in Business
Studies at the moment? Anybody?
No? Well, we're looking at famous
companies. This week, we are talking
about Coca Cola. Look at the bar
chart. Here, we can see the sales of
Coca Cola worldwide in 2000. For
example, sales in North America were
a little more than five billion bottles.
In Latin America, they were a little
more than four billion [PAUSE] bottles.

Teacher 5: OK. In Geography today, we're
looking at a new country. Brazil.
First, you need to turn to the map.
It's on page 45. Brazil is in green
on this map. As you can see,
Brazil is an enormous country. It
takes up half of the continent, that
is half of South [PAUSE] America.

Teacher 6: Today we are going to talk about
colours. In your books, you have a
photograph of a rainbow. Look at
the photograph. We see this effect
all the time, but can you explain
it? Why do we see all the colours
of the rainbow sometimes – red,
orange, yellow, green, blue, indigo
and [PAUSE] violet.

Presenter: 1:3

**Exercise D1. Listen to the
introduction to the lecture and
check your ideas.**

Lecturer: Today, I'm going to talk about learning. In particular, I'm going to look at learning at school. Firstly, what do students learn at school? I'm going to talk about the sort of information they learn. Secondly, *why* do they learn those items? I'm going to discuss the reasons for different items.

OK, so first, what do students learn at school? Well, of course, they have subjects – Maths, History, Geography and Science. But what sort of information do they learn in each subject? What knowledge do they learn? Firstly, they learn names and dates. For example, the names of famous people like John F. Kennedy, the President of the United States in the 1960s. Secondly, they learn about places – countries, like Italy, continents like Africa and so on. Finally, they learn important formulas, like the Pythagoras formula for right-angled triangles – c squared equals a squared plus b squared.

So students all over the world learn names and dates, they learn about places, and they learn famous formulas. We call this knowledge. In the past, students only learnt knowledge at school. Of course, students must also understand. So understanding is also an important part of school life. But, nowadays, students in many countries are also learning skills. What skills are you learning at the moment?

Presenter: 1:4

Exercise E. Listen. Number the items in the order that the lecturer mentions them.

Lecturer: So, nowadays, students learn knowledge and skills at school.

The skills help them in the real world. Firstly, children learn to read. Then they learn to write. Handwriting is still important, but, nowadays, keyboard skills are more important in many cases. So, secondly, we teach handwriting and then keyboard skills. As I said, we teach young children to read and to understand. But later, we teach them to read and evaluate. What does that mean? It means to think about information and ask the question: 'Is this true?' There is a lot of information on the Internet, but some of the information is not true. We must teach students to evaluate information. So that's the fourth skill – evaluating information. People must not believe everything they read. Finally, we teach students to communicate. Students need to give their ideas and to talk about themselves. They need to communicate in speech and in writing. Oh, I almost forgot. Working with other students. This is very important. Students must learn to work with other students and with adults. So, that's the last skill.

Presenter: 1:5

Lesson 2: Speaking

Exercise A2. Listen and check.

Voice: 1 Geography
2 History
3 Music
4 Mathematics
5 Science
6 Physical Education
7 Religious Studies
8 Literature
9 IT
10 Art

11 Business Studies
12 Psychology

Presenter: 1:6
Exercise B. Listen to some words. What's the subject?

Voice:
country	Geography
computer	IT
dates	History
football	Physical Education
landscape	Art
God	Religious Studies
novel	Literature
island	Geography
king	History
Bible	Religious Studies
song	Music
program	IT
laboratory	Science
map	Geography
numbers	Mathematics
customer	Business Studies
painting	Art
tennis	Physical Education
poem	Literature
printer	IT
singer	Music
continent	Geography
triangle	Mathematics
company	Business Studies

Presenter: 1:7
Exercise C1. Listen to the conversation.

Female: Are you at school or university?
Male: I'm at school. I'm in Year 12.
Female: What are you studying?
Male: I'm doing History, Psychology and Business Studies.
Female: Really? What are you doing in History at the moment?
Male: We're learning to evaluate information.
Female: What does that mean?
Male: We read something, then we say 'Is this true or false?'
Female: What's your favourite subject?
Male: I like Psychology.
Female: Why?
Male: Because it is important for me. I want to be a teacher.

Presenter: 1:8
Exercise C2. Listen and repeat.
[REPEAT OF 1:7]

Presenter: 1:9
Exercise D2. Listen and check.

Voice: learn to type
learn about graphs
learn to draw a graph
learn to play the guitar
learn about the Second World War
learn to write a business letter
learn about Brazil
learn to find countries on a map
learn to use the Internet safely
learn about spreadsheets

Presenter: 1:10
Exercise F. Listen to a student's talk.

Jane: Hello. My name's Jane Morris. I'm at university. I'm in the first year. I'm studying IT. I'm also doing Business Studies. At the moment in IT, we're learning about flow charts. We're learning to draw flow charts for simple actions. In Business Studies, we're learning about service industries, like banking and tourism. We're learning to write a business plan for a service industry.
I like IT because it is interesting. It is important for me because I want to be a computer programmer. I like Business Studies, too, because I want to start my own company.
OK. That's it. Thank you.

Presenter: 1:11

Lesson 3: Vocabulary and Pronunciation

Exercise A2. Listen to the students. They are describing the photos. Which ones are they talking about?

Student 1: a This photo is outside the university building. Maybe they are in a park. There are several students. Maybe they are working on an assignment together. Or maybe they are preparing a presentation. Two students are looking at their laptops. One student isn't working. He's sending a text message on his cellphone.

Student 2: b Well, there are two students. They're in a cafe or canteen. They aren't working, obviously. They're having coffee.

Student 3: c There's one student in this photo. I think she's a medical student or something like that. She's working in a laboratory. She's probably making up a solution.

Student 1: d There are two students in this photo. They are in a computer room. The teacher is explaining something and pointing at the computer screen. The students are listening carefully. Maybe the student at the front of the picture doesn't understand something.

Student 2: e There are two students in this photo. They're studying in a library. He's reading a book. And she's reading a book too.

Student 3: f This picture is outside. There's only one student. He's sitting under a tree. He's reading and studying.

Presenter: 1:12

Pronunciation Check. Listen and practise the pronunciation of the ~ing form of these verbs.

Voice: making
working
sending
listening
preparing
pointing

Presenter: 1:13

Listen to the sentences from Exercise B and practise.

Voices: 1 She's working in the laboratory. She's doing an experiment.

2 Two students are studying in the library. They're reading books.

3 Two students are sitting in the canteen. They aren't working. They're having coffee. They're smiling at the camera.

4 These students are preparing a presentation for a tutorial. One student isn't working. He's sending a text message. One girl's looking at the camera. Two students are working on their laptops. Maybe they are doing some research on the Internet.

5 This student is sitting under a tree. He's working hard on an assignment.

6 Two students are listening carefully to the teacher. The teacher's explaining something. She's pointing at the screen.

Presenter: 1:14

Exercise D1. Listen and check your answers.

A: Hi! Where are you going?

B: I'm on my way to the canteen.

A: Great. I'm going there too. Can we talk about the presentation?

B: Sure. But let's have some coffee first.

C: You're studying hard! Are you working on your assignment?

D: No, I'm not. I'm reading the article from the last lecture.

C: I read that last night. It's very interesting.

D: It's very difficult! Can you explain it to me?

Presenter: **1:15**
Exercise D2. Listen again. Notice the intonation in each question.
[REPEAT OF 1:14]

Presenter: **1:16**
Unit 2: Daily Life
Lesson 1: Listening
Exercise A. Listen and point.

Voices: a cellphone
a laptop
an mp3 player
a face-to-face conversation
a text message
an e-mail message
a Google page
a social networking site

Do you have your cellphone with you?
Do you have a laptop?
Do you have a good mp3 player?
Do you have many face-to-face conversations every day?
Can you send me a text message?
How many e-mails do you get every day?
Do you use Google for research?
What is your favourite social networking site?

Presenter: **1:17**
Exercise B. Listen to the first part of a Sociology lecture.

Lecturer: In Sociology this week, we're looking at the daily life of teenagers in the modern world. Today I'm going to look at teenagers and technology. Teenagers are living in the digital age. What does that mean? It means that teenagers use digital methods for communication. Digital methods use a computer in some way. Communication methods include e-mails, text messages and cellphone conversations. They also use digital methods for entertainment. Entertainment methods include mp3 players. Finally, they often use digital methods for research. Research methods include search engines like Google and they also include websites.

Presenter: **1:18**
Exercise C. Listen to the next part of the lecture. What does the lecturer say about teenagers? Tick one or more sentences.

Lecturer So this is the digital age. Teenagers in many countries use digital methods to communicate with their friends. They don't often talk to them face to face. And they don't often talk to them on the phone. Teenagers today communicate in a different way from their parents.

Presenter: **1:19**
Exercise D. Listen to the next part of the lecture. Write the number of minutes next to each bar.

Lecturer How long do teenagers spend on digital media every day? According to recent surveys, American teenagers spend, on average, 111 minutes every day texting friends. One hundred and eleven minutes. That's nearly two hours, every day. They spend another 45 minutes talking to their friends on their cellphones. So that's 156 minutes on their cellphones, texting and making voice calls. They also communicate with their friends by e-mail. That's another 22 minutes every day. Finally, they spend 12 minutes a day on social networking sites. So, American teenagers spend 190 minutes every day, on average, communicating with their friends on digital media. That's more than three hours.

Presenter: 1:20

Exercise E1. Listen and make notes in Table 1.

Lecturer: So American teenagers spend more than three hours every day communicating with friends. They use digital methods. Is this a good thing or a bad thing? Some people say it is good. Let's look at the advantages. Firstly, teenagers use digital methods to keep in touch with their friends. Sometimes their friends live in a different town or a different part of the city. But they can talk to them every day. Secondly, for teenagers, digital methods are like friends. They are friends in their pockets or handbags. They are friends in their laptop. They stop them feeling lonely. However, some people say that digital methods are a bad thing. Let's consider the disadvantages. Firstly, teenagers don't talk to people face to face. They don't learn this important skill for life. Secondly, digital methods get in the way of schoolwork and university work. Teenagers are texting and e-

mailing each other. They are not doing research. They are not doing homework. They are not doing assignments. What do you think?

Presenter: 1:21

Exercise E3. Listen to the whole lecture.

Lecturer: In Sociology this week, we're looking at the daily life of teenagers in the modern world. Today I'm going to look at teenagers and technology. Teenagers are living in the digital age. What does that mean? It means that teenagers use digital methods for communication. Digital methods use a computer in some way. Communication methods include e-mails, text messages and cellphone conversations. They also use digital methods for entertainment. Entertainment methods include mp3 players. Finally, they often use digital methods for research. Research methods include search engines like Google and they also include websites.

So this is the digital age. Teenagers in many countries use digital methods to communicate with their friends. They don't often talk to them face to face. And they don't often talk to them on the phone. Teenagers today communicate in a different way from their parents.

How long do teenagers spend on digital media every day? According to recent surveys, American teenagers spend, on average, 111 minutes every day texting friends. One hundred and eleven minutes. That's nearly two hours, every day. They spend another 45 minutes talking to their friends on their cellphones. So that's 156 minutes on their cellphones, texting and making voice calls. They also communicate with their friends by e-mail. That's another 22 minutes every day. Finally, they spend 12 minutes a day on social networking sites. So, American teenagers spend 190 minutes every day, on average, communicating with their friends on digital media. That's more than three hours. So American teenagers spend more than three hours every day communicating with friends. They use digital methods. Is this a good thing or a bad thing? Some people say it is good. Let's look at the advantages. Firstly, teenagers use digital methods to keep in touch with their friends. Sometimes their friends live in a different town or a different part of the city. But they can talk to them every day. Secondly, for teenagers, digital methods are like friends. They are friends in their pockets or handbags. They are friends in their laptop. They stop them feeling lonely. However, some people say that digital methods are a bad thing. Let's consider the disadvantages. Firstly, teenagers don't talk to people face to face. They don't learn this important skill for life. Secondly, digital methods get in the way of schoolwork and university work. Teenagers are texting and e-mailing each other. They are not doing research. They are not doing homework. They are not doing assignments. What do you think?

Presenter:	1:22

Lesson 2: Speaking

Skills Check 1. Listen to some times.

Voice:	1	quarter past six
	2	half past seven
	3	ten to eight
	4	eight o'clock
	5	five past nine
	6	twenty five past ten
	7	six fifteen
	8	seven thirty
	9	seven fifty
	10	eight
	11	nine o five
	12	ten twenty five

Presenter:	1:23

Exercise C. Listen to a talk by a university student in China.

Lian: My name is Lian. I am from Beijing. Beijing is the capital of China. I am a university student. I want to tell you about my daily life. In particular, I want to tell you about using digital communication in my daily life.

I always wake up at 6.30 and I get up immediately. I turn on my cellphone. I sometimes get text messages from my friends very early in the morning.

I wash and I get dressed and I go downstairs. At 7.00, I have breakfast. I don't listen to my mp3 player during breakfast.

At 7.30, I leave the house and catch the bus to the university. I always listen to music on the bus. I sometimes text my friends.

Lectures start at 8.00. I turn off my cellphone. Some people use their phones in lectures, but I don't. But I sometimes record lectures on my mp3 player.

I have lunch at 12.00. I talk to my

friends. I don't listen to my mp3 player. I go home at 12.30. I listen to music on the way home and I text my friends.

In the afternoon, I look at my notes. I turn on my laptop and I do research on the Internet. I use Google. I listen to music on my mp3 player and I work at the same time. Sometimes my friends call me about the assignments, but usually they send me texts.

At 6.00, I have dinner, then I go back to my laptop. I log on to a social networking site and I talk to my friends. We talk about university work and other things. At 9.00, I turn off my laptop and my cellphone. I go to bed and I go to sleep.

Presenter: 1:24

Lesson 3: Vocabulary and Pronunciation

Exercise A2. Listen and check your answers.

Voice: have a shower
clean my teeth
have a shave
put on my make up
get dressed
brush my hair
pack my bag
lock the door

Presenter: 1:25

Pronunciation Check. Listen and practise.

Voice: I get dressed.
I brush my hair.
He has a shave.
She puts on her make up.
We pack our bags.
They lock the door.
I take off my jacket.
I unpack my bag.
She unlocks the door.

Presenter: 1:26

Exercise C1. Listen.

A: When do you usually wake up?

B: At half past six.

A: Do you get up immediately?

B: No. I get up at about quarter to seven.

A: What do you usually have for breakfast?

B: I always have coffee and two pieces of toast.

A: How do you get to school?

B: Sometimes I walk and sometimes I go by car.

A: What time do you have lunch?

B: At quarter past one.

A: Do you ever sleep in the afternoon?

B: No, I don't. I never sleep in the afternoon.

Presenter: 1:27

Exercise C2. Listen and repeat.
[REPEAT OF 1:26]

Presenter: 1:28

Unit 3: Work and Business
Lesson 1: Listening

Exercise A. Listen and point.

Voices: bank
builder
factory
farm
shop
bus
sea
shop assistant
farmer
bus driver

Do you want to work in a shop?
Would you like to be a farmer?
Are you going to work for the government?
He loves the sea. He's a lifeguard.
He's a machine operator in a factory.
She's working in a bank at the

moment.

Every summer, I work on my uncle's farm.

I don't want to work outside, for example, on a building site.

Presenter: 1:29

Exercise B. Listen and match the employment sectors and the photographs.

Voice: She works in a bank. She's in finance.

They are builders. They're in the construction sector.

He works on a machine in a large factory. He's in manufacturing.

He grows crops and raises animals on a small farm. He's in agriculture.

He's a lifeguard on the beach. He's in the leisure industry.

She's a minister. She's a very important person in government.

He's a bus driver. He works in the transport sector.

She's a shop assistant. She's in retail.

Presenter: 1:30

Exercise C. Listen to part of a lecture about employment in the UK. Complete Table 1.

Lecturer: I'm going to talk to you today about employment sectors. Perhaps you are thinking already about work after university. Which sector do you want to work in? I'm going to tell you about employment sectors in the UK. Then I'm going to ask you to do some research into employment sectors in your country.

OK. So, first, where do most people work in the UK? According to a survey by Labour Market Trends in June 2004, most people in the UK work in the government sector. Does that seem strange? Remember. Most doctors and nurses work for the government. Most teachers in schools, colleges and universities work for the government. And of course, there are many clerks and typists in local government offices. Twenty-eight per cent of people in the UK work for the government in one way or another. Twenty-eight per cent.

In second place in the survey, we have the leisure and retail industries. Leisure and retail. Leisure means hotels and holiday travel. Retail means shops, of course, and supermarkets. Britain is a popular holiday destination and 20% of people in Britain work in hotels, restaurants and shops.

Finance is in third place. Sixteen per cent of people – that's one six – work in banks, insurance companies, etc.

So that's government first – 28%, leisure and retail second with 20% and finance third on 16%.

What's fourth? Agriculture perhaps? No. Not nowadays. At one time, most people in Britain worked on a farm, but now only 1% are in agriculture. Manufacturing is not very important now either, but still 15% work in that sector. After manufacturing, we have transport at 7% and construction at 6%. Other industries, like fishing, make up the remaining 7%.

So, from fourth down, we have manufacturing on 15%, transport 7%, construction 6% and agriculture just 1%.

Have a look at those figures for a few minutes. Do you think they are similar in your country?

Presenter: 1:31

Exercise D1. Listen and check.

Voice: A Cleaners, builders and farm workers are manual workers.

B People in charge of companies or offices are managers.

C Secretaries, typists and clerks are office workers.

D Doctors, lawyers and teachers are professionals.

Presenter: 1:32

Exercise D2. Listen to the next part of the talk. What does the speaker say about each type of job?

Lecturer: OK, we have heard about employment sectors. Now let's look at another important point about jobs. There are different kinds of jobs. What *kind* of job do you want to do? Are you going to be a manager? Managers often have interesting jobs. But they work long hours and they have a lot of responsibility. Or do you want to be a professional, like a doctor or a lawyer or a teacher? Professionals earn high salaries in most countries, but you must do many years of study. What about office work? Do you want to be an office worker? Some people think office jobs are boring, but they are often quite easy and you work in comfortable conditions. Finally, perhaps you would like to be a manual worker. Perhaps you want to work with your hands. Manual work is usually hard, but some people like working outside, and some people like making things.

What kind of worker do you want to be?

Presenter: 1:33

Exercise E2. Listen to the last part of the talk.

Lecturer: How easy is it to get each type of job? Well, the world is changing. At one time, nearly everyone was a manual worker. But what about today? It is difficult to get accurate figures for different kinds of jobs. But I have some information from the United States.

In the United States, there are about 120 million people with a job. Fifty million are manual workers. Fifty million – that's about 42% of the workforce. In second place, we have office workers. There are about 35 million office workers, which is 29% of the workforce. Next, we have professionals. They account for 22 million jobs which is 18%. Finally, there are managers. There are 13 million managers in the USA. That's 11% of the total workforce.

Presenter: 1:34

Lesson 2: Speaking

Pronunciation Check. Listen and repeat the sentences.

Voices: 1 I'd like to work in the retail sector.

2 I want to study agriculture.

3 I'm going to study finance.

4 She'd like to have a job in the leisure sector.

5 He wants to become a doctor.

6 Would you like to work in an office?

7 Are you going to work in the construction sector?

8 Does Adriana really want to be a tourist guide?

Presenter: 1:35

Exercise B. Listen to Paul and Jane. Which sector is good for Paul?

Jane: What kind of job would you like to do after college, Paul?

Paul: I don't know, really.

Jane: There's a flow chart in this magazine. It helps you choose an employment sector.

Paul: Show me.

Jane: No, I want to test it. I'll ask you some questions then I'll tell you a good sector for you.

Paul: Right.

Jane: First question. Would you like to work inside?

Paul: Yes.

Jane: OK. Second question. Would you like to meet new people?

Paul: What? In my job?

Jane: Yes.

Paul: Yes, I would.

Jane: Right. Third question. Would you like to travel?

Paul: Yes, definitely.

Jane: OK. It says: the leisure industry or the transport industry. Do you agree with that?

Paul: Mmm. I'm not sure about the transport industry, but I'd like to work in the leisure industry.

Presenter: 1:36

Exercise C. Listen to the introduction to a talk at the training day. What is the trainer going to talk about? Tick one subject.

Trainer: In this session, we are talking about job interviews. Sometimes people do badly in job interviews because they don't prepare. So, in this session, I'm going to talk about preparing for a job interview. You can prepare in many ways, but I'm only going to talk about one way. In a job interview, the interviewer often starts with 'Tell me about yourself'. We call this a presentation. You must speak for one or two minutes. You must prepare for this presentation. So that's the subject for this session.

Presenter: 1:37

Exercise D. Listen to the next part of the talk.

Trainer: OK. So let's look at some areas for your presentation. Firstly, you can talk about your background. This means your family and your home town or city. Maybe your nationality too.
Next, talk about your education. Tell the interviewers about your school and your university. Tell the interviewers about your subjects. Why did you choose your subjects? Which exams did you pass?
Thirdly, talk about any achievements. Maybe you learnt to play the piano or maybe you were captain of the football team. Finally, talk about your future career plans. What would you like to do in the future? Why?

Presenter: 1:38

Exercise E2. Listen and check.

Voices: I have a certificate in First Aid.
I have two brothers and one sister.
I passed the secondary certificate with 83%.
I want to work in the leisure industry.
I was head girl at my secondary school.
I went to secondary school in Rome.

I'd like to be a manager.

I'm from Recife in northern Brazil.

Presenter: **1:39**

Lesson 3: Vocabulary and
Pronunciation

**Exercise A2. Listen to the phrases
in the box. Where is the main
stress on each phrase?**

Voice: a job advertisement

a resume

an application letter

a job interview

Presenter: **1:40**

Exercise B2. Listen and check.

1

A: Did you see this job
   advertisement?

B: No, I didn't. What's it for?

A: Supastore is looking for a
   Trainee Manager.

B: Are you going to apply?

A: Yes, I think so.

2

A: Can you help me with my job
   application?

B: Sure. What's the problem?

A: They want my resume and a
   covering letter. What do I put
   in the letter?

B: Tell them about yourself, then
   tell them the reasons that you
   are applying for the job.

3

C: Thank you for coming to the
   interview.

A: Thank you for inviting me.

C: Let's start with some
   background information.

A: Certainly.

C: Tell me about yourself …

4

C: This is the manager of
   Supastore. We met yesterday
   at the interview.

A: Oh, yes. Hello.

C: Hi. We would like to offer you
   the job of Trainee Manager.

A: That's wonderful.

C: We want you to start in the
   Purchasing Department.

A: Yes, of course.

Presenter: **1:41**

**Exercise D2. Listen and check
your answers.**

Voice: apply application applicant

employ employment employer
employee employed unemployed

interview interview interviewer
interviewee

qualify qualification qualified
unqualified

train training trainer trainee
trained untrained

Presenter: **1:42**

Unit 4: Science and Nature
Lesson 1: Listening

**Exercise A. Listen. Which
photograph(s) can you see each
item in?**

Voices: trees

leaves

flowers

the sea

sand

the sky

clouds

snow

rocks

people

Presenter: 1:43

Exercise B. Listen to four descriptions by students.

Student 1: This photograph is from Russia. Um … Russia is in Europe and Asia. The photograph shows the city of St. Petersburg in winter. There's a lot of snow and the temperature is below freezing. In Europe, winter is December to February. But it can be much longer in St. Petersburg.

Student 2: This photo's from Barbados in the West Indies. As you can see, it's a beautiful day in summer. It's hot … um … and the sea is calm. There are only a few clouds in the sky.

Student 3: This photograph was taken in Holland. Holland is a small country in Europe. It's famous for its flowers. In the photograph, it's spring and we can see thousands of tulips, … um … red and yellow. In the northern hemisphere, spring starts in March and ends in May.

Student 4: This is a photograph of Vermont. Er … Vermont is in the east of the United States. People say it's the most beautiful place in the world in autumn. This photograph shows the lovely autumn colours in a forest. In Canada and the USA, people say *fall* and not *autumn*.

Presenter: 1:44

Exercise C. Listen to a short talk about seasons. Complete the table. Guess the spelling of each place name.

Lecturer: OK so most parts of the world have four seasons. For example, Islamabad, which is the capital of Pakistan, has a cold season, a hot season, a wet season and, lastly, a cool season. The cold season is from December … um … to the end of March. And … er … the hot season is from the beginning of April to June … yes … June. Now, the wet season is from July to September. And so, finally, the cool season starts in October and ends in November.

So that was Pakistan. However, some parts of the world only have [PAUSE] two seasons. For example, Baga, which is in the north of Nigeria, in Africa, has a dry season and a wet season. Um … the dry season is from October to April. And the wet season is from May to September.

Baga is in the northern hemisphere. But some places in the southern hemisphere also have two seasons. For example, Nazca in Peru [PAUSE] which is in South America, has a summer season and a winter season. The summer season is from December to March because Peru is in the southern hemisphere. And the winter season is from April to November. Now let's look at the seasons in …

Presenter: 1:45

Exercise E. Listen to the introduction to a lecture about climate.

Lecturer: Now, today, [PAUSE] we're going to talk about climate around the world. So, world climate. Firstly, I'll give you a … um … a definition of climate. Then I'm going to look at the main types of climate. OK, so first, what is climate? We all know the word *weather*. Rain, and wind and sun. Is climate the same as weather? No, it isn't. Weather is part of climate, but they are not the same. Climate is connected with a particular region. It is the normal weather in a particular region. But it is more than that. Most regions in the world have seasons. Two, three or four different times of the year. So we must look at the normal weather in each season: summer, winter, spring and autumn. And not just one year. We need data from many years. We must look for patterns over many years.

Presenter: 1:46
Exercise F. Listen to the main part of the lecture. Look at the key above.

Lecturer: Right. That's our definition. Now, let's look at the main climate types. [PAUSE] As I said, there are six main types. Let's start with the climate at the poles. It's called the … er … polar type. The area around the North Pole has a polar climate. That's northern Canada, Greenland, and the northern part of Europe and Russia. As you probably know already, the polar climate is very cold … and very dry.
Second, we have the continental climate. It is very common. Now, the continental climate is warmer than the polar climate. But it is still cold. And it is also humid. A humid climate has a lot of water in the atmosphere. The air is wet. So, that's the polar climate and the continental climate.
Next, we have the mild climate. Mild means not hot and not cold. The eastern states of the US have a mild climate. A lot of Europe has a mild climate and a few parts of southern Africa and southern and eastern Australia. [PAUSE] China

also has a mild climate.
The fourth climate type is called dry. Dry, in this case, means no rain, or not very much rain. We can find this climate in all the continents. It is in the western states of the USA and in the southern parts of South America. It's in large parts of Africa and Asia, and it is the climate of most of Australia … Of course, deserts have a dry climate, like the Sahara desert in North Africa. Dry climates are very hot in the day, but in winter, they are very cold at night.
The fifth climate type is called tropical. Why tropical? It is the climate in many areas between the tropics – the Tropic of Cancer north of the Equator and the Tropic of Capricorn south of the Equator. The tropical climate is hot, sometimes very hot. It is also humid.
Finally, we have the mountain climate. Mountains, of course, are high. Some mountains are very high. The height, or altitude of these mountains affects the climate. The highest mountains in the world are the Rockies in the west of the US, … um … the Andes in the west of South America, then the … er … Alps in the centre of Europe and, of course, the Himalayas in the north of India. In these mountain areas, it is colder than the rest of the region. Why? Because the area is high above sea level.

Presenter: 1:47
Exercise G. Listen to the summary. Number the next piece of information in each case.

Lecturer: So, to sum up. In this lecture, we have heard a definition of climate and [PAUSE]. So ... there is a polar climate at the North Pole and [PAUSE]. We talked about the continental climate. That is warmer than the polar climate, but [PAUSE]. Third, the mild climate. Mild means not hot and [PAUSE]. What's next? It's the dry climate. Now, um, dry climates have no rain, or [PAUSE]. Deserts are obviously dry climates. They are very hot in the day, but [PAUSE]. And now the fifth climate. The tropical climate. Tropical climates are between the Tropic of Cancer and [PAUSE]. Finally, there is the mountain climate. Mountain areas have a special climate because [PAUSE]. And so there we have our six climates ...

Presenter: 1:48
Listen and check.

Lecturer: So, to sum up. In this lecture, we have heard a definition of climate and information about climate types. So ... there is a polar climate at the North Pole and the South Pole. We talked about the continental climate. That is warmer than the polar climate, but it is still cold. Third, the mild climate. Mild means not hot and not cold. What's next? It's the dry climate. Now, um, dry climates have no rain, or not very much rain. Deserts are obviously dry climates. They are very hot in the day but very cold at night. And now the fifth climate. The tropical climate. Tropical climates are between the Tropic of Cancer and the Tropic of Capricorn. Finally,

there is the mountain climate. Mountain areas have a special climate because the land is very high. And so there we have our six climates ...

Presenter: 1:49
Lesson 2: Speaking
Exercise B. Listen to a tutor. Look at the handout on the right.

Tutor: Don't forget that we have our second tutorial on Wednesday ... what's the date? ... The 15th? Yes, Wednesday the 15th. It's at three o'clock. The topic this week is ... let me see ... 'How do humans adapt to their environment?' OK. So, think about that question and do some research before the tutorial. I want you to look at either the Inuit of Northern Canada, or the Masai of East Africa. Find out about their region and, in particular, research the geography of the region and the climate. OK, so that's next Wednesday 15th at three. How do humans adapt to their environment? See you then.

Presenter: 1:50
Exercise C. Listen to part of the tutorial. Make notes about the Inuit in the table on the right.

Tutor: Right. Anja. So what can you tell us about the Inuit?

Anja: OK, well, first, geography. They live in Northern Canada and in Greenland. The area is very flat and low. It is only a few metres above sea level. Some of it is an ice sheet.

Student 1: Sorry. What does that mean?

Anja: It's a large area of ice on top of the sea.

Tutor: OK. Go on.

Anja: Right. The Inuit live in a polar climate, so it is very cold. It snows from late August to April.

Tutor: Interesting.

Anja: Oh, I forgot to say. The temperature in winter sometimes goes down to minus 75.

Student 1: Sorry. What did you say?

Anja: Minus 75.

Student 2: Minus 75! That's freezing!

Tutor: What other livings things are in their environment?

Anja: Well, there are polar bears, seals and whales. There aren't any trees and there are only a few bushes.

Tutor: So how do they adapt to their environment?

Anja: Well, there are two main ways. Firstly, they have very thick clothes. They make coats and hats from fur. The fur comes from polar bears. And they make boots from seal skin. And secondly, they live in houses called igloos. They make the houses from ice, but they are very warm.

Teacher: Anything else?

Anja: Um. Yes, they use the dogs from the region. The dogs pull sledges on the snow.

Student 1: What are sledges?

Anja: They are carts, but they don't have wheels.

Presenter: 1:51

Lesson 3: Vocabulary and Pronunciation

Exercise D1. Listen. Follow the conversation in the pictures.

A: Hi. How are things?

B: They're good, thanks.

A: What's the weather like with you?

B: Oh, it's great. Very warm and sunny.

A: You're lucky! It's terrible here.

B: Why? Is it raining?

A: Yes, it is. It's pouring!

B: Oh dear.

Presenter: 1:52

Exercise D2. Listen and repeat. [REPEAT OF 1:51]

Presenter: 1:53

Exercise E. Listen to some conversations. Answer the questions about each conversation.

1

A: What's the weather forecast for the weekend?

B: Well, it's going to be cloudy on Saturday.

A: Oh, no! What about Sunday?

B: It's going to rain, I'm afraid.

A: Typical! It always rains at the weekend!

2

A: Does it often snow in London?

B: No, it doesn't, but it often rains.

A: What's the average temperature in the summer?

B: I'm not sure. About 17 degrees, I think.

3

A: Bulent. What's the climate like in your country?

B: Well, in the summer, it's hot, and there isn't much rain.

A: What about in the autumn or the winter?

B: In the winter, it's sometimes very cold.

4

A: It's getting colder.

B: Yes, it is. Winter's nearly here.

A: It's dark at five in the evening now.

B: I hate the winter.

Presenter: 1:54

Pronunciation Check. Listen and check.

Voice: What's the forecast for the weekend?
What's the average temperature in the summer?
What about in the autumn?
It's dark at five in the evening now.

Presenter: 1:55

Skills Check. Listen to the start of some conversations.

A: It's nice today.
B: Yes, it is. Lovely weather for …

A: Is it raining outside?
B: I'm afraid so. It's horrible, but I think …

A: What a lovely day!
B: It is. It's beautiful! Much better than …

Presenter: 2:1

Unit 5: The Physical World
Lesson 1: Listening
Exercise A2. Listen and check.

Voices: planets
Jupiter
Mars
Mercury
Neptune
Saturn
The Earth
The Sun
Uranus
Venus

Presenter: 2:2

Exercise A3. Listen and point to the item in each case.

Voice: 1 It's next to the Sun.
2 It's between Mercury and the Earth.
3 It's next to Neptune.

4 It's between Jupiter and Uranus.
5 It's between Mars and Venus.

Presenter: 2:3

Exercise A4. Listen and complete each sentence with a name from Figure 1.

Voice: 1 At the centre of the solar system is [PAUSE] the Sun.
2 The nearest planet to the Sun is called [PAUSE] Mercury.
3 The fourth planet from the Sun is called [PAUSE] Mars.
4 There is a large planet with rings. It is called [PAUSE] Saturn.
5 The largest planet in our solar system is [PAUSE] Jupiter.
6 The planet between Neptune and Saturn is called [PAUSE] Uranus.
7 The planet next to Mercury is called [PAUSE] Venus.
8 The smallest planet is called [PAUSE] Mercury.

Presenter: 2:4

Exercise B2. Listen and check.

Voice: the Earth
the crust
the inner core
the mantle
the outer core

Presenter: 2:5

Exercise B3. Listen and point to the part in each case.

Voice: It's at the centre of the Earth.
It's above the inner core.
It's below the crust.
It's between the inner core and the mantle.

Presenter: 2:6

Exercise B4. Listen and complete each sentence with a word or phrase from Figure 2.

Voice: 1 The top part of the Earth is called [PAUSE] the crust.

2 The centre of the Earth is called [PAUSE] the inner core.

3 Next to the inner core is the [PAUSE] outer core.

4 Between the crust and the outer core, there is a layer called [PAUSE] the mantle.

5 The mantle is above the [PAUSE] outer core.

6 The mantle is below the [PAUSE] crust.

Presenter: 2:7

Exercise C. Listen and write the answer.

Voice: 1 Which is the nearest planet to the Sun?

2 Which planet is between the Earth and Jupiter?

3 Which is the largest planet in the solar system?

4 What is the inner part of the Earth called?

5 Which layer is between the crust and the outer core?

6 Which layer is below the mantle?

Presenter: 2:8

Exercise D. Listen to the introduction to the lecture.

Lecturer: Today, we're going to talk about the Solar System. In particular, you're going to hear about two natural events in the Solar System. First, I'll talk about an eclipse of the Sun and then I'll describe an eclipse of the Moon. Don't worry about the word *eclipse* at the moment. I'll explain it in the lecture.

Presenter: 2:9

Exercise E. Listen to the first part of the lecture.

Lecturer: 1 Now, I've given you a couple of photographs and two …

2 Can you look at the photograph and the diagram on the …

3 What does the photograph …

4 Well, of course, it shows the …

5 But in front of the Sun, we can see part of the …

6 The Moon is moving between the Earth and the Sun. We call this natural event an …

7 This is an eclipse of the Sun. Eclipses of the Sun happen every 18 months somewhere on the …

8 But this is not a total eclipse. The Moon is not covering the Sun …

9 We call this kind of eclipse, partial, from the word …

10 On average, total eclipses only happen once every 100 …

11 Look at the diagram under the …

12 The red arrows show the way that the Moon …

Presenter: 2:10

Exercise E2. Listen again to this part and check.

Lecturer: 1 Now, I've given you a couple of photographs and two diagrams.

2 Can you look at the photograph and the diagram on the left.

3 What does the photograph show?

4 Well, of course, it shows the Sun.

5 But in front of the Sun, we can see part of the Moon.

6 The Moon is moving between the Earth and the Sun. We call this natural event an eclipse.

7 This is an eclipse of the Sun. Eclipses of the Sun happen every 18 months somewhere on the Earth.

8 But this is not a total eclipse. The Moon is not covering the Sun completely.

9 We call this kind of eclipse, partial, from the word *part*.

10 On average, total eclipses only happen once every 100 years.

11 Look at the diagram under the photograph.

12 The red arrows show the way that the Moon moves.

Presenter: 2:11

Exercise F2. Listen to the second part of the lecture and check your answers.

Lecturer: OK. So that's an eclipse of the Sun. Now look at the photograph and the diagram on the right. OK, everyone got that? Now, this photograph shows an eclipse of the [PAUSE] Moon. So, what's happening here? Well, the Earth is moving between the Sun and the Moon. On average, three eclipses of the Moon happen every year somewhere on the Earth. Total eclipses happen nearly as often as partial eclipses.

Why do eclipses happen? The answer is simple. They happen because the Moon goes round the Earth and the Earth goes round the Sun. Sometimes, the Earth is between the Moon and the Sun. We call this an eclipse of the Moon. And of course, sometimes the Moon is between the Sun and the Earth. We call this an eclipse of the Sun. Do other planets in our solar system have eclipses?

Presenter: 2:12

Exercise G. Listen to some sentences about Figures 3 and 4. Which figure is the speaker talking about in each case?

Lecturer: 1 The diagram shows an eclipse of the Sun.

2 The diagram shows an eclipse of the Moon.

3 The Moon is between the Earth and the Sun.

4 The Moon is in front of the Sun.

5 The Moon is behind the Earth.

6 The Earth is between the Sun and the Moon.

7 The Earth is in front of the Moon.

Presenter: 2:13

Lesson 2: Speaking

Exercise B. Listen to the start of a lecture. Complete the introduction on the right.

Lecturer: Today, I'm going to talk to you about the history of the continents. I don't mean the human history. I mean the physical history. Where were the continents million of years ago? According to scientists, they weren't in the same places as today. They were in different places, and they looked very different too.

Presenter: 2:14

Exercise C. Listen to the main part of the lecture and look at Figures 2, 3 and 4 on the opposite page.

Lecturer: So, we need to go back millions of years. Two hundred and fifty million years ago, in fact. Then, there was only one continent. Scientists called it [PAUSE] Pangea. The word Pangea means all lands. Look at the figure. It is difficult to see today's continents. You can see this continent went from the north to the south. Around the continent, there was one ocean, called Panthalassa. This word, of course, means all seas.

We now move forward about 50 million years. We are now looking at about 200 million years ago. At this time in the Earth's history, there were two continents. Scientists called the continent in the northern hemisphere [PAUSE] Laurasia and the continent in the southern hemisphere [PAUSE] Gondwanaland. That's Laurasia in the north and Gondwanaland in the south. The present continents of Europe, North America and … er … Asia were in Laurasia, and South America, Africa, Oceania and, lastly, Antarctica were in Gondwanaland. And … um … the subcontinent of India was also in Gondwanaland.

And now we have quite a big step forward in time. Eighty-five million years ago, there were, at last, seven continents. Look at the figure. You can see Europe and Asia were together in the northeast. Now this is interesting, North America and South America were separate in the west. And you can see Africa was in the centre. Antarctica was below Africa, with Australia to the east. Notice that India was a separate continent. It was east of Africa. So the figure is still not the map of the world that we recognize today.

Presenter: 2:15
Exercise D. Listen to the last part and look again at Figure 4.

Lecturer: So how did the continents reach their modern position? Well, for the next 50 million years, the continents kept moving. North America moved away from Europe and Asia. It moved to the west. And South America? That continent moved away from Africa to the northwest. Now can you see Antarctica in the figure? Antarctica moved to the south. Africa, India and Australia moved to the northeast. So all three moved in the same direction. But India kept moving towards Asia. Finally, India crashed into Asia. What happened? Well, something very exciting. The huge Himalayan mountains appeared with the highest mountain in the world, Mount Everest. The Himalayas are the youngest mountain range on Earth.

How can the continents move? Why do they move? Well, the continents are on the crust of the Earth. The crust is solid rock. But, as you know, the crust is on the mantle, and the mantle is liquid rock. The crust moves very, very slowly on top of the mantle. Like a stick or piece of wood on water.

Presenter: 2:16
Exercise E1. Listen and check your answers.

S1: There was only one continent 250 million years ago.
S2: That's right. What was it called?
S1: Pangea, I think. It means 'all lands'.

S1: What happened to Pangea 200 million years ago?
S2: It split into two parts.
S1: Can you remember the names?
S2: Yes, Laurasia and Gondwanaland.

S1: What was the world like 85 million years ago?
S2: Well, there were seven continents, but they were in different places.

S1: What changed in the next 50 million years?

S2: Um, North America moved away from Europe and Asia and … er … India moved towards Asia.

S1: How can the continents move?

S2: Well, the continents are on the crust and the crust is above the mantle.

S1: Right. And what's important about the mantle?

S2: It's not solid. It's liquid.

Presenter: 2:17
Lesson 3: Vocabulary and Pronunciation
Pronunciation Check 1. Listen and check your pronunciation.

Voice: The hottest
The largest
The lightest
The coldest
The nearest
The hottest planet is Venus.
The largest content is Asia.
Which suitcase is the lightest?
January is usually the coldest month.
Heathrow is the nearest airport to London.

Presenter: 2:18
Pronunciation Check 2. Listen and repeat each sentence.

Voice: 1 The cafe is next to the bank.
2 The lecture theatre is on the floor below.
3 He usually comes out of the lecture a bit late.
4 Why's she walking away from us?
5 Look at the figure under the photo.
6 I've parked my car behind the sports centre.

7 We're going into town about 9 o'clock.
8 The book's on the shelf above you.

Presenter: 2:19
Exercise E2. Listen and check your answers.

A: Where's the nearest bank?

B: It's near the park. Go down the hill.

A: Towards the city centre?

B: No, away from the centre. Go under the bridge and round the corner. It's between the post office and the supermarket.

A: Is there a car park?

B: Yes. The car park is behind the bank.

B: Can you park in the street?

A: Sometimes. There are some spaces in front of the supermarket.

Presenter: 2:20
Review
Lesson 1: Listening
Exercise B. Listen to the introduction to a lecture about the man in the drawing. Number the topics in order.

Lecturer: I'm going to talk to you today about a man called Pythagoras. Firstly, I'm going to tell you a little about his life. Then I'm going to talk about his famous formula. Finally, I'll describe a real life way of using his formula.

Presenter: 2:21
Exercise C. Listen to the first part of the lecture. Number the next piece of information in each case.

Lecturer: OK. So first, Pythagoras. Who was he? Pythagoras was born over 2,500 years ago in about 570 BCE. His hometown was Samos in

Greece, but [PAUSE]. He left at the age of 40 because [PAUSE]. He went to a place called Croton in Italy. He studied Science, Literature and the Solar System, but [PAUSE]. He started a school in Croton because [PAUSE]. He became famous in the town and [PAUSE]. However, some important people didn't like the ideas of Pythagoras and [PAUSE]. Pythagoras died in about 495 BCE at the age of about 75.

Presenter: 2:22

Exercise D. Listen to the second part of the lecture.

Lecturer: Pythagoras is famous today because he worked out something very important about triangles. Well, not all triangles. One particular kind of triangle. This kind of triangle is called a right-angled triangle. Look at the diagram. The yellow triangle is a right-angled triangle. It has three sides: a, b and c. The angle between side a and side b is a right angle. In other words, it is 90 degrees. OK. So, what did Pythagoras discover? Look at the blue squares on side a. How many squares are there? Count them. Write the number down. Now look at side b. Look at the green squares. Count the green squares. Write that number down. Finally, look at side c. Count the red squares. Write that number down. Now we can say that the area of the blue squares is a times a or a squared. We write that as *a* with a little number 2. So the area of the green squares is b^2 and the area of the red squares is c^2. Work out the areas of the blue squares, the

green squares and the red squares. Add the areas of the blue squares and the green squares together. It is the same as the area of the red squares. So what is Pythagoras' formula or theorem?

Presenter: 2:23

Exercise E. Listen to the third part of the lecture.

Lecturer: The Pythagoras formula or theorem says c squared equals a squared plus b squared. It is interesting, but is it useful? In fact, people use the formula all the time in everyday life. For example, imagine a building is on fire. The firemen need a ladder to get to the roof of the building. But what size ladder do they need? Let's say the building is eight metres high. They want to put the bottom of the ladder six metres from the building. Use Pythagoras' theorem to work out the answer.

Presenter: 2:24

Exercise F. Listen to the stressed syllables of some words from the lecture. Number the word in each case.

Voice: 1 sub
2 por
3 an
4 cribe
5 buil
6 re
7 for
8 a
9 in
10 tri
11 fa
12 sci

Lesson 2: Speaking

Exercise B2. Listen and check your answers.

A: It's cold today.

B: Yes, it is.

A: And it's raining. I hate rain.

B: Actually, I like it. But I don't like cold weather.

A: It was warmer yesterday.

B: Yes. Warm and sunny.

A: Are you at the university?

B: Yes, I am. I'm in the first year. What about you?

A: I'm in the first year, too.

B: What are you studying?

A: English Literature.

B: Why are you doing that?

A: I want to be an English teacher. And you?

B: I'm going to be an engineer.

A: Hi. How are you?

B: Fine, thanks.

A: Do you always have lunch in the canteen?

B: No, I sometimes bring sandwiches from home.

A: Where do you live?

B: In North Street. Next to the supermarket. What about you?

A: I live near London Road. There are some flats behind the bank.

A: What time do you finish today?

B: The lecture ends at 3.45.

A: Are you going to catch the bus to town?

B: Yes. There's one at about 4.00.

A: It's at 4.05, actually. I sometimes get that bus.

Lesson 3: Vocabulary and Pronunciation

Exercise B2. Listen and check.

Voice:
1	autumn	draw
2	bear	hair
3	brush	sunny
4	builder	skill
5	climate	high
6	cloudy	shower
7	east	deep
8	explain	wake
9	leisure	west
10	region	season

Exercise C2. Listen and check.

Voice:
1 prepare
2 explain
3 triangle
4 compulsory
5 application
6 yesterday
7 communicate
8 reference
9 interesting
10 trainee
11 independent
12 advertisement
13 tropical
14 temperature
15 between
16 agriculture

Presenter: **1:1**

Unit 1: Education

Listening and Speaking

Exercise B3. Listen and check.

Voices: 1 A: When do children begin pre-school in your country?

B: They begin at three or four.

2 A: Do all children go to pre-school?

B: No. Most children start school at five.

3 A: When do children leave primary school?

B: Most children leave at 11. A few children change schools at 12 or 13.

4 A: Where do they go?

B: To a secondary school, from 11 to 18.

5 A: Do all children study the same subjects?

B: Yes, they do. For the first three years of secondary school. Then they can choose.

6 A: When can children leave school?

B: When they are 16.

7 A: Do most children leave school then?

B: No. Some children leave then, but most children stay at school for another two years.

8 A: What about university or college?

B: Nowadays, most teenagers go on to university or college.

Presenter: **1:2**

Exercise D2. Listen and check your answers.

Student 1: I'm an IT student. I'm really enjoying my course. At the moment, we're studying website design. I'm writing an assignment about it. My tutor is really nice. She's helping me a lot with my assignment at the moment.

Student 2: I'm studying Sociology. There are six students in my tutor group. Two students are studying education and sociology. Two students are preparing a presentation with me at the moment. They are helping me a lot. They have really good ideas.

Student 3: I'm taking tourism. I'm not doing much work at the moment. I'm not feeling well. My friends are taking notes for me this week because I can't go to lectures.

Presenter: **1:3**

Unit 2: Daily Life

Listening and Speaking

Exercise A3. Listen and check.

Voice: a He comes from Japan.

b He studies Economics.

c He likes going to the sports centre.

d He sends texts and e-mails.

e He uses social networking sites.

f He makes voice calls.

Presenter: **1:4**

Exercise B2. Listen and check.

Voice: 1 Where does he live?

2 We go home by bus.

3 I don't understand this word.

4 What do you do in the evenings?

5 I like my lectures very much.

6 She doesn't go to the lectures.

7 I catch the bus at 7.55.

8 I meet my tutor once a week.

9 John sends a lot of texts on his phone.

10 My friend has sandwiches every day.

Presenter: 1:5

Exercise C2. Listen and check.

Voices:
1 I'm not a teacher. I'm a student.
2 Beijing is in China.
3 We aren't going to a lecture today – it's Sunday!
4 What time does the lecture start?
5 My father doesn't send texts because he doesn't understand his cellphone.
6 How long do teenagers spend on computers?
7 They don't want to do the assignments – they are too difficult!
8 Where's the bus? I'm late!

Presenter: 1:6

Exercise D2. Listen and check.

Voices:
1 I don't spend a lot of time on social networking sites.
2 My boss doesn't send a lot of e-mails everyday.
3 Teenagers don't communicate in the same way as their parents.
4 Teenagers don't talk a lot face-to-face.
5 Beatriz doesn't live in a big house.
6 I don't watch TV every evening.
7 I don't always come late.
8 He doesn't usually park his car near the supermarket.
9 My mother isn't always tired in the evenings.
10 You don't always give me lots of food!

Presenter: 1:7

Unit 3: Work and Business
Listening and Speaking
Exercise A. Listen and complete the flow chart.

Teacher: OK. Today, in IT, we're going to make a flow chart. Then we're going to use the flow chart. We're going to use it to choose a type of job for you.

Right. Look at the flow chart. Find the first question. It says 'work with hands'. That means: *Do you want to work with your hands?* You can answer *yes* or *no*, of course. The yes answer goes to a rectangular box. What do we write in here? Do you want to work with your hands? *Yes, I do.* So we write in here 'Manual worker'. Can you write that in the box now.

OK. Look at the next decision box, the diamond shape. It says 'study for a long time' so that is the question: *Do you want to study for a long time?* Once again, the *yes* answer goes to a rectangular box. What do we write this time? Do you want to study for a long time? *Yes, I do.* So we write in here 'Professional'. Can you do that? Write 'Professional' in the rectangular box.

Finally, the last decision. 'Be in charge' which means: *Do you want to be in charge?* If you answer *yes*, you want to be ... a manager. So can you write 'manager' in the box.

OK. That's it. You have the complete flow chart.

Presenter: 1:8

Exercise C. Listen and check.

Voice:
1 high salary
2 long hours
3 manual worker
4 interesting job
5 secondary certificate
6 career plan
7 leisure industry

8 job advertisement

9 organized person

10 bank clerk

Presenter: 1:9

Exercise D. Listen and check.

Voices:
1 He wants to work with his hands.

2 She would like to be a teacher.

3 They are going to go to university.

4 I want an interesting job.

5 I don't want to be in charge.

6 Do you want to work outside?

7 Would you like to be a manager?

8 Are you going to go on to university?

9 What is he going to do after university?

10 Where is she going to live?

Presenter: 1:10

Exercise E. Listen. Number the best word or phrase to complete the questions.

Voices:
1 Do you work inside or …

2 Do you work with your …

3 Are you in …

4 Do you meet …

5 Do you work for …

6 Do you use mathematics in …

7 Do you work with …

8 Do you sell …

9 Do you travel …

10 Is your job …

11 Do you get a lot …

12 Do you work in …

Presenter: 1:11

Unit 4: Science and Nature
Listening and Speaking
Exercise B1. Listen to the first part. Label the map above. Guess the spellings.

Voice: Several people have asked us here at *World News*: 'How do you choose the cities to give the weather for?' Well, we have chosen the major capital cities of the world. We have weather stations in every continent except Antarctica. In North America, we usually give weather information for Washington and Mexico City. [PAUSE] In South America, we only have one city report, from Buenos Aires or B.A. as it is sometimes called. [PAUSE] I forgot to say, mmm, the weather stations all collect information about temperature, and wind direction and speed. As well as rain, of course. And air pressure. Now where was I? Yes, Europe. Now in Europe, we give weather conditions for London in the east, [PAUSE] Helsinki in the north, [PAUSE] and Moscow in the west. [PAUSE] We have weather observers in Athens in the south [PAUSE].

We have three weather stations in Africa. In the north of the continent, we have one in Cairo. [PAUSE] That's a very large one. We also have one in Riyadh [PAUSE] and there is one in the south of the continent, in Pretoria. [PAUSE]

Finally, we have three stations in Asia. In India, we have a station in the capital, New Delhi. [PAUSE] We have one in Beijing in China [PAUSE] and one in Tokyo. [PAUSE] Oh, and of course, we have a station in Australia, in the capital, Canberra.

These days, some stations are automatic, but they are still checked regularly …

Presenter: 1:12

Exercise B2. Listen to the next part.

Voice: What do weather stations look like? Well, of course, some are very large and have a lot of expensive equipment. But some are very simple. You can set up a weather station in your garden, for example, or at your school or university. It's easy and it's very cheap. You only need an open space away from buildings and trees. Why? Because buildings give off heat, and buildings and trees provide too much shade.

OK. What's next? Well, you need a white box for your equipment. It must be white because that reflects heat. Put your thermometer and other equipment inside. Then you must take readings regularly, twice a day, and always at the same time. That's really important. You can record the information for two or three months, but it's best to collect the information for two or three years. Then you can see differences and patterns from year to year.

What can you do with the data? Well, you can compare two types of weather, for example, wind direction and the amount of rain. Or you can compare your data with information from another local weather station.

Presenter: 1:13

Exercise C2. Listen and check.

Voice:
1	trees	season
2	autumn	August
3	cloud	flower
4	snow	cold
5	country	summer
6	weather	terrible
7	humid	tutor
8	tropical	rock
9	adapt	average
10	ice	climate

Presenter: 1:14

Exercise D2. Listen and check.

Voices:
1 It's really cold today. They say it's going to snow.

2 It's really cloudy today. Maybe it will rain.

3 In the States, autumn is called 'fall'.

4 In Britain, the weather is often cold, wet and humid.

5 Which country are you from?

6 What was the weather like on your holiday?

7 It was terrible. It rained nearly every day.

8 Do they have a dry season in the rainforest?

9 Animals can't adapt quickly to the environment.

10 I tripped over a rock.

Presenter: 1:15

Exercise E2. Listen and check.

A: Now, what can you tell us about the Sherpa people?

B: Well, first, some geography. They live near the Himalayan mountains in Nepal. It's the biggest mountain range in the world. Some come from China and India.

C: Sorry. What does *range* mean?

B: It's a group of mountains.

C: OK. Thanks. Go on.

A: What is the weather like?

B: Well, Nepal has two different climates. There's a mountain climate in the mountains, of course. But most of the country is tropical.

A: Interesting.

B: Oh, I forgot to say. Nepal has four seasons. In the wet season, they can have 375 millimetres of rain.

C: Anything else?

B: There are many animals – yaks, deer and wolves. They also have tigers, rhinos, snow leopards, pandas and elephants. But their numbers are very small.

A: How do they adapt to their environment?

B: The Sherpa people live at a very high altitude in the summer. But in winter, they go down to the lower parts of the country.

Presenter: 1:16
Unit 5: The Physical World
Listening and Speaking
Exercise A2. Listen to the first part of the talk. Write the information in Table 1.

Voice: OK. Last week we talked about the Inner Planets. This week, the Outer Planets. There are four outer planets. The first planet is Jupiter. It is 778 million kilometres from the Sun. Jupiter has a diameter of 143,000 kilometres. It takes twelve Earth years to go round the Sun. But it turns very quickly. One day on Jupiter lasts just ten Earth hours. What about the weight? Well, Jupiter is very large. It is 318 times the size of the Earth. Yes, 318. It's also very cold. The temperature doesn't change very much. It is always around minus 150 degrees Celsius. As you know, Earth has one moon. Well, Jupiter has 16. Some of the moons are very big. The Babylonians discovered Jupiter in about 2000 BCE, that's over 4,000 years ago. Now, let's look at Saturn. Saturn

is further from the Sun, of course. In fact, it is nearly twice as far. It's 1,427 million kilometres. That's 1,427. It's about the same size as Jupiter. The diameter is 120,000 kilometres. It takes longer than Jupiter to go round the Sun – 29 Earth years in fact. But it turns at about the same speed. One day on Saturn is 10.6 hours. It's lighter than Jupiter – 95 times the weight of the Earth. It's colder than Jupiter, at minus 180 degrees Celsius. Finally, moons. Saturn has 18. That's two more than Jupiter. The Babylonians also discovered Saturn in 2000 BCE. OK. You can find out the information for the other planets.

Presenter: 1:17
Exercise A4. Listen to the second part. Label Figure 2 with words from the box above.

Voice: Now, I want to talk about the parts of each planet. Firstly, Jupiter. In the middle of the planet is the core. It is solid. So, solid core, then above the core is solid hydrogen. Finally, the top part of the planet is liquid hydrogen. Secondly, Saturn. The core of Saturn is rock and ice – that's rock and ice, then above the core is solid hydrogen like Jupiter, then liquid hydrogen, also like Jupiter. OK, what about Uranus and Neptune? They have exactly the same composition. In the middle, a solid core, above the core, water, and above the water, methane. Oh, sorry, between the water and the methane, there is a layer of ammonia. So that's methane at the top, ammonia under the methane and then water at the bottom.

Presenter: 1:18

Exercise B. Listen and check.

Voice:
1 Uranus is 2,871 million kilometres from the Sun.
2 Neptune has a diameter of 50,000 kilometres.
3 Jupiter goes round the Sun in twelve Earth years.
4 One day on Uranus is shorter than an Earth day.
5 Saturn is much heavier than the Earth.
6 The temperature on Neptune is minus 210 degrees Celsius.
7 Neptune has eight moons.
8 A man called Herschel discovered Uranus in 1781.

Presenter: 1:19

Exercise C. Listen and check.

Voice:
1 The largest planet is Jupiter.
2 The farthest planet from the Sun is Neptune.
3 Jupiter has the shortest day and the shortest year.
4 Neptune is heavier than Uranus.
5 The heaviest planet is Jupiter.
6 The lightest planet is Uranus.
7 Uranus is between Saturn and Neptune.
8 The hottest planet is Jupiter.
9 Saturn is farther from the Sun than Jupiter.
10 The longest day is on Uranus.

Presenter: 1:20

Exercise D. Listen. Number the best word or phrase to complete each sentence about the history of the continents.

Voice:
1 Where were the continents million of years ...
2 They weren't in the same place as ...
3 According to scientists, they were in different ...
4 They looked very different ...
5 Two hundred and fifty million years ago, there was only one ...
6 This continent went from the north to the ...
7 Around the continent, there was one ...
8 About 200 million years ago, there were two ...
9 Then about 85 million years ago, the two continents split into seven ...
10 For the next 50 million years, the continents kept ...
11 For example, North America moved away from Europe and Asia. It moved to the ...
12 The continents are still moving today. What will the world look like in 50 million years ...

Presenter: 1:21

Listen to the complete sentences and check.

Voice:
1 Where were the continents million of years ago?
2 They weren't in the same place as today.
3 According to scientists, they were in different places.
4 They looked very different too.
5 Two hundred and fifty million years ago, there was only one continent.
6 This continent went from the north to the south.
7 Around the continent, there was one ocean.
8 About 200 million years ago, there were two continents.
9 Then about 85 million years ago, the two continents split into seven parts.

10 For the next 50 million years, the continents kept moving.

11 For example, North America moved away from Europe and Asia. It moved to the west.

12 The continents are still moving today. What will the world look like in 50 million years' time?

Presenter: **1:22**

Review

Listening and Speaking

Exercise A. Listen and tick the sentence you hear.

Voices:
1 We are doing triangles in Maths at the moment.

2 We did flow charts in IT last week.

3 He always plays football in the evenings.

4 I'm not going to leave school next year.

5 It is very cold in Antarctica so it doesn't rain.

6 Winter in North America is from November to February.

7 Polar bears live in Russia, Greenland and Canada.

8 The deepest lake in the world is Lake Baikal.

Presenter: **1:23**

Exercise B. Listen and check your answers.

Voices:
1 What do you want to be after university?

2 What are you studying at the moment?

3 What do you do in the summer?

4 What do you usually have for lunch?

5 What qualifications do you have?

6 What will the weather be like tomorrow?

7 Is it going to rain?

8 What's the average temperature in your country?

Presenter: **1:24**

Exercise C. Listen and check your answers.

Voices:
1 I'm reading a good book at the moment.

2 Where are you going?

3 She often gets angry.

4 Do you turn off your phone during lectures?

5 Can you help me with my job application?

6 I'd like to work in a hotel.

7 What's the weather like in your country in the winter?

8 Some animals are more protected than other animals.

9 John Couch Adams discovered Neptune 165 years ago.

10 The mantle is between the outer core and the crust.

Presenter: **1:25**

Exercise D1. Listen to the introduction. Number the topics in today's talk in order.

Lecturer: Good morning everyone. OK, at the moment in History we're looking at the 19th century. Last week, we discussed Europe in the 1800s and next week, we're going to talk about China and Japan. But, today, I'm going to talk a little bit about the United States. Now, of course, the American Civil War was the big event in the States in the 19th century. So, in this lecture, I'm going to tell you briefly about that – the American Civil war from 1861 to 1865. Probably the most important person in the war was Abraham Lincoln, so I'm going to start with his life. Then we'll look at the problems in the States in the 1860s. Finally, I'm going to tell you about the results of the American Civil War. What happened in the States after the war. OK, so first …

Presenter: 1:26

Exercise D2. Listen to the next part of the talk. Choose the best way to complete each sentence.

Lecturer:

1 This term in History, we are studying America in the 19th …

2 We are going to look first at the life of Abraham Lincoln, the 16th President of …

3 He was born in 1809 in a small …

4 He did not have much education. He hardly ever went to …

5 He had several jobs as a young man, for example, farm worker, shopkeeper and …

6 He became President in …

7 The American Civil War began in the same …

8 In 1863, he made a famous speech about …

9 He said: Government should be of the people, by the people, for the …

10 In 1865, Lincoln was shot and, about 10 hours later, he …

Word list

	Unit		Unit
above *(prep)*	5	dangerous *(adj)*	4
achievement *(n)*	3	deep *(adj)*	5
advantage *(n)*	2	depth *(n)*	5
advertisement *(n)*	3	diagram *(n)*	1
affect *(v)*	4	difficult *(adj)*	4
ago *(adv)*	5	disadvantage *(n)*	2
agriculture *(n)*	3	dog *(n)*	4
alarm *(n)*	2	draw *(v)*	1
altitude *(n)*	4	dry *(adj)*	4
always *(adv)*	2	east *(adj)*	5
applicant *(n)*	3	effect *(n)*	4
application *(n)*	3	employ *(v)*	3
Art *(n)*	1	employee *(n)*	3
assignment *(n)*	1	employer *(n)*	3
autumn *(n)*	4	employment *(n)*	3
away from *(prep)*	5	evaluating *(v)*	1
background *(n)*	3	exercise *(n)*	1
bank *(n)*	3	experiment *(n)*	1
bank clerk *(n)*	3	explain *(v)*	1
bear *(n)*	4	explanation *(n)*	3
beautiful *(adj)*	4	factory *(n)*	3
behind *(prep)*	5	far *(adv)*	5
below *(prep)*	5	farm *(n)*	3
between *(prep)*	5	farmer *(n)*	3
boring *(adj)*	3	fast *(adj)*	4
bottom *(adj)*	5	finance *(n)*	3
brush my hair *(v)*	2	flow chart *(n)*	1
brush my teeth *(v)*	2	foggy *(n)*	4
builder *(n)*	3	friendly *(adj)*	3
bus *(n)*	3	fur *(n)*	4
bus driver *(n)*	3	Geography *(n)*	1
Business Studies *(n)*	1	get dressed *(v)*	2
catch the bus *(v)*	2	get home *(v)*	2
cellphone *(n)*	2	get up *(v)*	2
climate *(n)*	4	go to bed *(v)*	2
cloudy *(adj)*	4	go to sleep *(v)*	2
cold *(adj)*	4	government *(n)*	3
comfortable *(adj)*	3	have a shave *(v)*	2
communicating *(v)*	1	have a shower *(v)*	2
compulsory *(adj)*	1	hemisphere *(n)*	5
computer *(n)*	3	high *(adj)*	4
confident *(adj)*	3	History *(n)*	1
construction *(n)*	3	hobby *(n)*	3
co-operative *(adj)*	3	hot *(adj)*	4

humid *(adj)*	4	often *(adv)*	2
imaginative *(adj)*	3	old *(adj)*	5
in front of *(prep)*	5	organized *(adj)*	3
in the centre *(prep)*	5	out of *(prep)*	5
in the corner *(prep)*	5	over *(prep)*	5
independent *(adj)*	3	pack my bag *(v)*	2
interest *(n)*	3	patient *(adj)*	3
interview *(n/v)*	3	paw *(n)*	4
into *(prep)*	5	personality *(n)*	3
IT *(n)*	1	photograph *(n)*	1
Jupiter *(n)*	5	Physical Education *(n)*	1
keyboard skills *(n)*	1	pie chart *(n)*	1
kind *(adj)*	3	planet *(n)*	5
knowledge *(n)*	1	prepare *(v)*	1
laptop *(n)*	2	primary school *(n)*	1
leave home *(v)*	2	professional *(n)*	3
left *(adv)*	5	protected *(v)*	4
leg *(n)*	4	Psychology *(n)*	1
leisure *(n)*	3	punctual *(adj)*	3
length *(n)*	5	put on make up *(v)*	2
lightning *(n)*	4	rain *(v)*	4
lips *(n)*	4	region *(n)*	4
liquid *(n)*	5	Religious Studies *(n)*	1
Literature *(n)*	1	responsibility *(n)*	3
lock the door *(v)*	2	retail *(n)*	3
low *(adj)*	4	right *(adv)*	5
manager *(n)*	3	rock *(n)*	5
manual worker *(n)*	3	salary *(n)*	3
manufacturing *(n)*	3	Saturn *(n)*	5
Mars *(n)*	5	Science *(n)*	1
Mathematics *(n)*	1	sea *(n)*	3
Mercury *(n)*	5	season *(n)*	4
mild *(adj)*	4	secondary school *(n)*	1
modern *(adj)*	4	shop *(n)*	3
mp3 player *(n)*	2	shop assistant *(n)*	3
Music *(n)*	1	skill *(n)*	1
near *(adv)*	5	skin *(n)*	4
neck *(n)*	4	smart *(adj)*	3
Neptune *(n)*	5	social networking site *(n)*	2
never *(adv)*	2	solid *(n)*	5
next to *(prep)*	5	sometimes *(adv)*	2
north *(adj)*	5	south *(adj)*	5
nose *(n)*	4	spring *(n)*	4
nursery school *(n)*	1	storm *(n)*	4
office worker *(n)*	3	subject (school) *(n)*	1

summer *(n)*	4
sunny *(adj)*	4
temperature *(n)*	4
text *(n)*	1
texting *(v)*	2
the Earth *(n)*	5
the Moon *(n)*	5
the Solar System *(n)*	5
the Sun *(n)*	5
top *(adj)*	5
towards *(prep)*	5
trainee *(n)*	3
transport *(n)*	3
tropical *(adj)*	4
tutorial *(n)*	1
under *(prep)*	5
Uranus *(n)*	5
usually *(adv)*	2
valley *(n)*	4
Venus *(n)*	5
voice call *(n)*	2
wake up *(v)*	2
warm *(adj)*	4
website *(n)*	2
weight *(n)*	4
west *(adj)*	5
wet *(adj)*	4
wide *(adj)*	5
width *(n)*	5
winter *(n)*	4
young *(adj)*	5